Transformation comes when the kingdom [...] less than the rule of Christ in absolutely [...] lives and our communal lives. This book is a call for a return to the biblical worldview, in which there is no separation between secular and sacred, physical and spiritual, or evangelism and social justice. In this book, Scott Allen reveals the neo-Gnosticism that has crept into many Christians' thinking today and calls us to be "re-minded" into a wholistic understanding and practice of the whole reign of Christ, over the whole of life, according to the whole Word of God, for the sake of the whole world.

Joel Hogan
Director of International Ministries, Christian Reformed World Mission

Christianity is personal, but it is never private. If Jesus Christ is who he is portrayed as in Scripture, he is Lord over every aspect of creation and human life. Unfortunately, a deep seated dualism continues to plague Christians and the church, fragmenting our view of reality and dividing our allegiances between things "sacred" and "secular." Scott Allen's book destroys this dualism and shows how discipleship involves all of our lives, loves, and relationships. I pray this book gains a wide reading. Its message is desperately needed.

John Stonestreet
Summit Ministries and Breakpoint

In Great Commission ministry, word and work must go together. Losing one or the other distorts beyond recognition the good news Jesus taught and embodied. Perhaps the greater temptation for many Christians today is to emphasize work without word, leading to powerless liberalism. But others among us may think they have successfully communicated the good news while failing to live it out for those who have not only ears to hear but eyes to see (and stomachs to fill). In any case, missionaries, ministry leaders, pastors, and people in the pews need to absorb and act upon the bracing and potentially life-changing message of this book.

Stan Guthrie
Editor at large, *Christianity Today*; author of *All That Jesus Asks*

It is exciting to read a Bible study that offers a wholistic view of all of creation. With wisdom and through experience, Scott Allen points readers to view all of life (mind, body, and soul) as a unified whole.

Kim Moreland
The Chuck Colson Center for Christian Worldview

The false division between the sacred and the secular has done much to debilitate the world-changing impact God intended for the church. Breaking down this artificial wall is the essential first step towards freeing the church to again be God's agent of transformation in its society. That is what this book does in a way that is profound but also simple and understandable.

Joel Huyser
Cofounder, The Nehemiah Center Managua, Nicaragua

This is an extraordinary work in its concise conceptual exposition, practical implementation, and potential to transform individuals, cultures, and societies. The call for a wholehearted Christianity needs to be heard and responded to for an effective witness in today's world. I heartily recommend this book.

Iman Santoso
General Coordinator, Transformation Connection Indonesia

Christians today are faced with the stark reality that the church has lost its influence in the community and the marketplace. In this masterful study Scott Allen explains why this has happened and how it can be turned around. Allen debunks the myth that Christianity is only relevant in the private worlds of the church and the individual and provides practical examples of how an integrated Kingdom view of the world can lead Christians to become agents of social transformation. This is a message which is extremely timely for the days in which we live.

Derek Brown
Director, Rediscovering the Kingdom, Brisbane, Australia

As a college instructor and campus minister at a major public university, every day I see the tragic results of the dualism that has so infected our churches. Scott Allen gives me—and all of us—a wonderfully helpful tool by which we can root out this habit of separating sacred and secular, public and private. In its place, he helps us plant the biblical concept of wholism, which, when biblically understood, is bound to produce rich intellectual and practical fruit in the lives of my students—and yours.

Robert Osburn, PhD
Executive Director, Wilberforce Academy; lecturer, University of Minnesota

BEYOND
THE <u>*SACRED-SECULAR*</u>
DIVIDE

A CALL TO
WHOLISTIC LIFE
AND MINISTRY

Scott D. Allen

YWAM Publishing
Seattle, Washington

Disciple
Nations
Alliance

Founded by:
Harvest and Food for
the Hungry International

YWAM Publishing is the publishing ministry of Youth With A Mission. Youth With A Mission (YWAM) is an international missionary organization of Christians from many denominations dedicated to presenting Jesus Christ to this generation. To this end, YWAM has focused its efforts in three main areas: (1) training and equipping believers for their part in fulfilling the Great Commission (Matthew 28:19), (2) personal evangelism, and (3) mercy ministry (medical and relief work).

For a free catalog of books and materials, call (425) 771-1153 or (800) 922-2143. Visit us online at www.ywampublishing.com.

Beyond the Sacred-Secular Divide: A Call to Wholistic Life and Ministry
Copyright © 2011 by Scott D. Allen

Published by YWAM Publishing
a ministry of Youth With A Mission
P.O. Box 55787, Seattle, WA 98155

First printing 2011

The introduction to Session 6, "Wholistic Ministry Essentials," is adapted from the article "Arturo Cuba's Ministry among the Pokomchi in Guatemala," Disciple Nations Alliance, Inc., 2004. Used by permission.

ISBN 978-1-57658-518-4

Printed in the United States of America.

Kingdom Lifestyle Bible Studies

God's Remarkable Plan for the Nations
God's Unshakable Kingdom
The Worldview of the Kingdom of God
Beyond the Sacred-Secular Divide

Acknowledgments

This project has truly been a team effort. Many thanks to Randy Hoag, former president of Food for the Hungry International and founder of Vision of a Community Fellowship, for his inspiration in developing this series and for his encouragement along the way. A debt of gratitude also goes to Judith Couchman and Sarah Gammill for their expert assistance with editing and proofreading. Several others contributed valuable insights in shaping the content of these lessons. Among these are our friends and colleagues Karla Tesch, Shirley Gowdy, Raaj Mondol, Buck Deines, Nathan Sandahl, Cleiton and Eli Oliveira, Bob Hedlund, and many other coworkers at Harvest and Food for the Hungry that have taught, inspired, and encouraged us over the years. Finally, a special thanks to Tom Bragg, Warren Walsh, Ryan Davis, and the entire team at YWAM Publishing for believing and investing in this project. We are honored to co-labor with such wonderful and committed brothers and sisters in Christ. *Coram Deo!*

Contents

≈ Foreword

Greetings from a fellow pilgrim! I am so pleased that you are beginning this Bible study. My passion is to see people growing in their relationship with King Jesus and his kingdom. I pray that this book and learning process will be such a blessing to you.

The Kingdom Lifestyle series is based on the analogy of a tree. The Bible often uses the metaphor of a fruitful tree to describe a healthy Christian life. Jesus said, "[It] is to my Father's glory, that you bear much fruit, showing yourselves to be my disciples" (John 15:8). Psalm 1 describes a blessed man as one who "is like a tree planted by streams of water, which yields its fruit in season and whose leaf does not wither. Whatever he does prospers" (v. 3). The "streams of water" represent God's Word, or "the law of the LORD" (v. 2).

So it is with our lives. To bear abundant fruit, we need to be rooted in God's Word. Not only are we to delight in God's Word and meditate on it (Ps. 1:2), but we must apply it. The apostle James warns, "Do not merely listen to the word, and so deceive yourselves. Do what it says" (James 1:22). In the strength that Christ provides, we are to conform every aspect of our lives to God's Word. It should shape our relationships with Christ, our vocational lives, our relationships with family members and fellow believers, and our ministries to our communities, nations, and the world.

That is what the Kingdom Lifestyle series is all about. It's about helping you deepen your relationship with the awesome, glorious God who is King of the universe, and increase your knowledge of his powerful Word. It's about assisting you in living out every facet of your life based on this relationship and knowledge. It's about helping you to carry it outward as you serve as "salt and light" (Matt. 5:13–16) in your community, nation, and the world. Ultimately, it's about bearing good fruit to the glory of God. No life can compare to the joyful, peace-filled, purposeful life lived for God, in his strength and according to his Word.

I am not only excited about the rich content of this series; I am also excited about the method. I am convinced that people learn best in small groups and by putting what they learn into practice. We were not created to grow alone. That's why each book is specially designed for use by small groups. If you are not already part of one, I encourage you to find a small group of brothers or sisters in Christ who you can pray with and who can encourage you as you learn and apply the lessons contained in this book.

May grace and joy abound in your life.

Serving the King and the kingdom together,

Randy Hoag
Founder, Vision of a Community Fellowship
www.vocf.net

About This Study

In this study, you'll learn about the concept of wholism and how it applies to our lives as followers of Jesus and also to our ministries. You can study by yourself or with a small group. There are six sessions in this study.

Theme of Each Session

Session 1. We'll define the concept of wholism and discover that it is a deeply biblical idea. We'll look at examples of how it is reflected in Scripture.

Session 2. We'll address a significant problem that Christians have faced through the centuries—a divided mind, leading to a divided life. We'll see how this mental dualism leads to a separation between the "spiritual" parts of life, such as faith, worship, and church attendance, and the "secular" parts of life, such as career and family life.

Session 3. We'll explore what a wholistic life looks like. We'll discover that a wholistic life is one of integrity, where faith in Christ impacts every part of our lives, and where we desire to glorify God in both private and public life, including family life, our careers, and even simple things like eating and drinking.

Session 4. Turning our attention to Christian ministry, we'll discover that a wholistic ministry is one that understands that God is Lord over *everything*. It also understands the comprehensive impact of the Fall as well as God's big agenda to bring hope and healing to everything affected by the Fall "through [Christ's] blood, shed on the cross" (Col. 1:20).

Session 5. We'll look at how the divided mindset destructively influences Christian ministry and missions. It subdivides God's comprehensive redemptive plan into "spiritual" and "unspiritual" parts. When this occurs, evangelism is wrongly separated from social ministry, such as concern and care for the needs of the poor and broken.

Session 6. We'll explore six essentials to practicing a truly wholistic ministry.

Sections of Each Session

Key Words to Know. After the opening narrative, each session includes discussion of some of the key words found in the session. In addition to reading the provided definitions, you may wish to use additional resources, such as a Bible dictionary or commentary, for further study of these terms. Understanding these words will help you get the most out of the study.

Key Verses to Read. After the discussion of key words, you'll find a key Scripture passage for the session. Carefully read the quotation and answer the questions after it. These key verses provide a biblical framework for the central teaching of each session. Whether you're leading or participating in a small group or studying alone, you can consult the suggested responses for each session's Key Verses to Read questions in the Study Notes section at the end of the book. Not all questions have a "right" or "wrong" answer, but these suggestions will help stimulate your thinking.

Biblical Insights. This narrative section is the heart of each session. Carefully read it, taking notes as you go along. As you read, highlight meaningful or important points and write down questions that come to mind.

Discovery Questions. This section is designed to take you into God's Word for a deeper understanding of the material covered in the Biblical Insights section. Suggested responses to these questions can be found in the Study Notes at the back of the book.

Key Points to Remember. This section briefly summarizes the key points for each session.

Closing Thoughts. This section provides a wrap-up of the session, designed to transition from the main body of the session to the personal application that follows.

Personal Application. Here's where the study gets personal. These questions are designed to help you reflect on your own life and experiences and move you toward personal application.

If you're leading a small group through this study, before beginning please read the Leader's Guide. Guidelines are provided that will help you enhance your group's effectiveness.

Please join us as we delve into Scripture and explore the deeply biblical concept of wholism, discovering how this idea can profoundly change your life and ministry. When we seek God with all our mind, body, and soul and seek to do his will in every part of our life, we become God's coworkers in his expanding kingdom and bring glory to his name.

The Power of an Undivided Life

The Bible reveals God as the all-powerful creator of everything. The Old Testament states that the Spirit of God was present when the heavens and the earth were created (Gen. 1:1–2), and the New Testament explains further that God the Father created all things "by" and "for" his Son, Jesus Christ (Col. 1:16). The triune God—Father, Son, and Spirit—is the Supreme Ruler over all creation (Ps. 24:1; Matt. 28:18) who orders and holds together the entire cosmos (Col. 1:17). He is not neutral toward or disinterested in his creation; he loves and delights in it (Gen. 1:31).

But all is not as it should be. Sin entered God's good creation. The Bible reveals sin not as an isolated spiritual ailment but as something that has radically disordered the cosmos (Gen. 3:17–18; Rom. 8:19–22). The Bible also reveals that God is working to redeem the fallen cosmos. The redemption that God provides through Jesus will result in a new heaven and a new earth (Rev. 21:1–2), not an abstract, spiritual heaven where saved human souls dwell. Jesus *is* our savior and redeemer, but he is also much more. He is the savior of the world, the redeemer of the entire cosmos (John 3:16)!

Christianity, when seen in this all-encompassing light, is not so much a religion but a comprehensive view of the universe. And it is the only view that aligns with reality as God has revealed it in his Word. The apostle Paul expresses this view in his letter to the church at Colosse. About Jesus he writes:

> He is the image of the invisible God, the firstborn over all creation. For by him all things were created: things in heaven and on earth, visible and invisible, whether thrones or powers or rulers or authorities; all things were created by him and for him. He is before all things, and in him all things hold together. . . . For God was pleased to have all his fullness dwell in him, and through him to reconcile to himself all things, whether things on earth or things in heaven, by making peace through his blood, shed on the cross.
>
> —*Colossians 1:15–17, 19–20*

Here Paul presents us with an all-encompassing Christian view of the universe: the phrases "all things" and "all creation" appear in the passage six times. Centuries after Paul lived, the great Dutch statesman and theologian Abraham Kuyper (1837–1920) expressed this same all-inclusive Christian worldview this way: "There is not a square inch of the universe over which King Jesus does not claim, 'Mine!'"[1]

The Church Today

Yet for many Christians today this comprehensive view of reality has been obscured. Many divide the world into mutually exclusive compartments: one is labeled "sacred" and has to do with the spiritual life and eternal things, and everything else goes into a "secular" compartment. For those who hold this divided view of reality, the consequences are profound. While they may trust Jesus as their spiritual savior, they also may fail to honor him as Lord over all areas of life. An invisible line divides their personal faith in Christ (along with church attendance, worship, prayer, and Bible study) from other areas of life such as work, leisure time, or care for the physical body. The day-to-day "secular" activities are assumed to be of little concern to God. As a result, Christianity is narrowed down to a scheme for spiritual salvation only. The cross is a ticket to heaven and little more.

When this divided view of reality takes hold within a church, it results in the separation of the church from its surrounding culture. Sunday worship services are seen as more important than weekday duties. "Full-time Christian service" is valued more than pursuits in the arts, law, politics, social services, care for the physical needs of the poor, and so on. The core doctrines of the Bible are seen as unconnected to culture and civic life. As a result, the church is sealed off from society in a Christian ghetto, with its own subculture of language, media, and entertainment. Rather than actively discipling the nations as Christ commanded (Matt. 28:18–20), the church becomes impotent and ineffective in impacting culture. Ironically, when the church does not seek to impact society, the values and dominant beliefs of the surrounding culture begin to influence and shape it.

Despite the loss of a biblical worldview in much of the church today, there is cause for great hope. God is at work in our generation. He is active around the world, leading his bride back to a comprehensive, undivided understanding of reality. He is reminding his followers that he is Lord not merely of some limited spiritual realm—he is Lord over all! He created the spiritual and the physical realms and cares for both equally. He seeks to be glorified not only in church buildings but also in homes, schools, businesses, courthouses, and the houses of government. Furthermore, he is reminding his bride that while he passionately and actively seeks and saves lost people trapped in sin (1 Tim. 2:4), his redemptive plan is even grander. He is redeeming all things distorted through the Fall (Col. 1:19–20). It is this all-encompassing redemptive agenda in which God calls his church to participate with him.

Wholism

Today a new word is proving useful in directing Christians back to a comprehensive, undivided mindset—*wholism*. Though this word is relatively new, the idea behind it is not. Wholism derives from the root word *whole* and is used to describe whole systems made up of multiple interconnected parts that function together. Think of your life as an example. Different parts of your life include your family life, your career, your spiritual life, recreation, and so on. A divided mindset will separate these parts into sacred and secular categories. A wholistic mindset will seek to glorify God in all areas of life, recognizing that God is concerned with the whole of your life and all that you do. Think also of Christian ministry. Some ministries focus on evangelism, others on discipleship, and still others on providing care for the poor and needy. A divided mindset will separate these activities into higher and lower categories. A wholistic mindset sees them as equally essential parts of the total ministry of advancing God's kingdom on earth.

The concept of wholism is both liberating and challenging. It holds the power to free us from a debilitating mental dualism. It provides a fresh, faith-expanding perspective that leads to newfound freedom to enjoy human life in all its wonder. It opens the door for us to take new interest and delight in God's magnificent creation. It enables us to explore vocational alternatives outside "full-time Christian service" and still know that we are serving and glorifying God. As whole churches embrace this perspective, they escape from the Christian ghetto and infiltrate and transform the surrounding culture through the power of God's Word lived out in human flesh.

Yet wholism is challenging because it requires that our faith inform our entire lives. When we truly grasp wholism, we realize we can no longer withhold certain segments of our lives from God. Jesus wants our lives—every part of them—to glorify him. He wants us to join him in advancing his kingdom in all areas of culture and society. For those who have been trapped within a divided mindset, this might seem like a scary and radical step. Yet Jesus promises that when we join him, our burden will be easy and our yoke will be light. The responsibility of advancing the kingdom belongs to God, yet he gives us—you and me—the privilege of working with him. When we accept this role as God's coworkers, he supplies the strength we need to do things we could never do on our own.

⤳ Understanding Wholism

When scientists peer outward into the vast universe, what do they see? According to scholar Patrick Glynn, they observe a universe with countless interdependent parts or systems, all working together in such amazing harmony that "the existence of life is something for which the entire universe appears to have been intricately fine-tuned from the start."[1]

When scientists look inward at the universe within a living cell, what do they see? According to biochemist Michael Behe, they view highly complex machines made of molecules. Behe explains:

> Molecular machines haul cargo from one place in the cell to another along "highways" made of other molecules, while still others act as cables, ropes, and pulleys to hold the cell in shape. Machines turn cellular switches on and off, sometimes killing the cell or causing it to grow. Solar-powered machines capture the energy of photons and store it in chemicals. Electrical machines allow current to flow through nerves. Manufacturing machines build other

molecular machines, as well as themselves. Cells swim using machines, copy themselves with machinery, ingest food with machinery. In short, highly sophisticated . . . machines control every cellular process. Thus the details of life are finely calibrated, and the machinery of life is enormously complex.[2]

Numerous systems, Behe further explains, thrive within living cells "composed of several parts, all of which contribute to the function [of the whole system]. . . . The removal of any of the parts causes the system to effectively cease functioning."[3]

Throughout the twentieth century, botanist Charles Darwin (1809–1882) dominated science with his popular view that all life forms arose by chance in a random universe. New scientific discoveries strongly challenge this theory. Far from being random and chaotic, the universe consists of interacting wholes, each made of interdependent parts, all working in harmony. Examples include a single cell, the human body, an ecosystem, and the solar system. This is powerful evidence of a Designer. When we observe the beauty and complexity of creation—the millions of parts working together with amazing precision and harmony—we can proclaim God's greatness with the writer of Psalm 104:24: "How many are your works, O LORD! In wisdom you made them all." God's creation is wholistic.

While the word *wholism* does not appear in Scripture, the concept is expounded throughout. Understanding it and applying it to our lives and ministries is critical for faithful Christian living. In this session we will define wholism and discover how and where it appears throughout Scripture.

KEY WORDS TO KNOW
What Is Wholism?

Wholism

Wholism is the theory or idea that the parts of a whole must be understood in relationship to the whole. It emphasizes the whole and the interdependence of the parts rather than the parts in and of themselves. The word was first used by early twentieth century scientists to describe the interconnected functioning of the universe. It is now used in other fields, including philosophy, psychology, and ecology. In this study the word is used to describe a Christian conception of human life lived out as God designed it.[4]

KEY VERSES TO READ

One Body, Many Parts

> The body is a unit, though it is made up of many parts; and though all its parts are many, they form one body. So it is with Christ. . . . God has combined the members of the body . . . so that there should be no division in the body, but that its parts should have equal concern for each other.
>
> —*1 Corinthians 12:12, 24–25*

1. What body is the apostle Paul describing in the above passage? See 1 Corinthians 12:27.

   _____

   _____

2. According to 1 Corinthians 12:28, what are the parts of this body?

   _____

   _____

   _____

3. How is the body designed to function?

   _____

   _____

BIBLICAL INSIGHTS
Wholism Revealed in Scripture

The idea of wholism has become very popular today. The adjective *wholistic* (or *holistic*) is applied to everything from medicine to management to ministry. Because New Age practitioners in the West frequently use the term, many associate it with pantheism and Eastern mysticism. As a result, some Christians are wary of the concept and tend to avoid it. Yet wholism is a profoundly biblical idea that needs to shape the mindset of Christians if they are to grow spiritually and have effective ministries. To think wholistically is to grasp the relationship between the parts and the whole. In these six sessions we will explore this important concept and its application to life and ministry.

The Church

We find this parts-and-whole thinking on display in the apostle Paul's description of the church in 1 Corinthians 12. The church, according to Paul, is a single entity, the "body of Christ," which consists of many parts (v. 12). He compares the church to the human body—another wholistic system—to illustrate. Human bodies have many interdependent parts, such as the eyes, feet, and ears. Paul explains, "If the whole body were an eye, where would the sense of hearing be? If the whole body were an ear, where would the sense of smell be? But in fact God has arranged the parts in the body, every one of them, just as he wanted them to be. If they were all one part, where would the body be? As it is, *there are many parts, but one body*" (1 Cor. 12:17–19, emphasis added). Paul describes the parts of the church as different offices (or roles) and gifts held by Christ's followers. "And in the church God has appointed first of all apostles, second prophets, third teachers, then workers of miracles, also those having gifts of healing, those able to help others, those with gifts of administration, and those speaking in different kinds of tongues" (1 Cor. 12:28).

The church universal is wholistic: it is the body of Christ directed by one Spirit, yet made of many parts. It is composed of individual members, each equipped with different gifts, banded together in local congregations.

Each of these local expressions is likewise a functioning system within the whole, with each member contributing his or her gifts to its health and effectiveness. Both on a local and on a global scale, we need one another to function as Christ's body in the world.

God and Reality

The ultimate source and sustainer of creation is God. He encompasses all of reality; nothing in the universe exists or could exist apart from him. To understand God we must recognize both the whole and the parts of his nature; that is, we must understand him wholistically. The Bible reveals God as tripersonal. According to theologian J. I. Packer, the doctrine of the Trinity affirms that "the one God ('He') is also, and equally, 'they,' and 'they' are always together and always cooperating" to unfold a plan of redemption for creation.[5] Throughout the course of history as recorded in the Bible, we see the work of one God in three persons—Father, Son, and Holy Spirit.

Christian author and scholar Nancy Pearcey describes the Trinity as "the Rosetta Stone of Christian social thought." She writes, "The human race was created in the image of God, who is three Persons so intimately related as to constitute one Godhead . . . *one in being* and *three in person*. God is not 'really' one deity, who appears in three modes: nor is God 'really' three deities, which would be polytheism. Instead, both oneness and threeness are equally real, equally ultimate, and equally basic and integral to God's nature."[6] We cannot speak of either the Father or the Son or the Holy Spirit as being more important than the others, nor can we take away one and still retain a true understanding of God. Likewise, we cannot understand reality or the various parts that make up the universe apart from God. To think correctly about God—about ultimate reality— we need to think wholistically.

The Bible

The Bible is wholistic. The whole is a unified story that describes the eternal existence and character of God, the origin and nature of the universe, the source of evil, the meaning and purpose of human life, and the ultimate goal of history. The Bible comprises sixty-six individual books made up of smaller sections and stories. Different authors penned these books, including Moses, King David, various prophets, and the apostles Paul and Peter, each using dramatically different styles (narrative history, poetry, music lyrics, personal letters, and others) written in multiple languages (mainly Hebrew and Greek) over the course of hundreds of years. But the Holy Spirit wove together this wide variety of writings to form a single story—the story of God and his unfolding redemptive plan in history. To subtract any part of the Bible would mean compromising the integrity of the whole. The parts are interdependent and equally important to the overall narrative.

God created a universe full of this whole-and-parts pattern. For Christians, and ultimately for all people, the concept of wholism is foundational to our understanding of the universe. We must think wholistically to understand God, Jesus, creation, the Bible, our society, our ministries, and ourselves.

DISCOVERY QUESTIONS
Seeing the Forest and the Trees

In the Bible, truth is often multifaceted and finely balanced. Rather than "this" or "that," truth is sometimes "both." We often encounter the truth as a greater whole with different parts held in balance. Open your Bible to explore some examples of this.

1. First look at Christians' witness in the world. According to Ephesians 4:15–16, what parts make up Christian witness as a whole?

   _____

   _____

2. What happens when we lose the balance between truth and love in our Christian witness?

   _____

   _____

   _____

3. Look next at ministry. According to Matthew 9:35, what parts make up Christlike ministry as a whole?

   _____

   _____

4. What happens when we lose the balance in our ministry between teaching/preaching and compassionate care for the broken and hurting?

   _____

   _____

   _____

5. Now consider God's character. According to Exodus 34:5–7, what parts make up God's character as a whole?

   _____

   _____

   _____

6. What happens when we lose the balance between compassion/grace/love and holiness/justice/wrath in our conception of God?

   _____

   _____

   _____

7. Think about the Christian lifestyle. According to Romans 1:17 and James 2:14–17, what should be essential parts of the Christian lifestyle?

   _____

   _____

8. What happens when we lose the balance between faith and good deeds?

   _____

   _____

   _____

KEY POINTS TO REMEMBER
The Whole and Its Parts

1. Wholism is the idea that the parts must be understood in relationship to the whole. This concept is found throughout the Bible. We must learn to think wholistically to grow in our faith and have effective ministries.
2. God created a universe of astounding diversity and complexity. Countless parts make up his creation, and each part contributes to the function of the whole.
3. The universal church is wholistic. The body of Christ is a single entity consisting of many equally important offices, roles, gifts, and local expressions.
4. God is wholistic. He is a complex unity of Father, Son, and Holy Spirit. Each of the three persons of the Godhead plays an essential role in God's redemptive plan.
5. The Bible is wholistic. It presents the overarching story of God's redemptive plan in history. Its parts (individual books and stories) are interdependent and equally important to the larger narrative.

CLOSING THOUGHTS
A Beautiful Balance

Thinking wholistically is not easy or automatic. It requires that we hold two or more parts in balance within the context of a greater whole. Sometimes these parts seem contradictory. How can Jesus be fully God and fully man? How can God be both one and three? As history has shown, problems arise when Christians focus on one aspect of life or belief to the neglect of others. When we fail to hold the parts in balance—if we fail to think wholistically—we miss the full truth contained in Scripture.

Truth is finely balanced. It functions like a mobile above the crib of an infant. With all the parts in place, it moves with beauty and symmetry. But remove one part and the entire mobile collapses. In the Christian life, the interdependent parts include law and grace, human freedom and

God's sovereignty, the present and future aspects of God's kingdom, evangelism and social action, and so on. Rather than representing uncompromising opposites, these parts provide the framework for Christian life and belief. When Christians stress one part at the expense of another, they lose the fullness of God's truth and the church divides and weakens. For the strength and health of the worldwide church, we must regain a wholistic understanding of life.

PERSONAL APPLICATION
Are You in Balance?

In the discovery questions, we looked at areas in Scripture where truth is finely balanced. Let's review these again, but this time reflect on our own lives.

1. For each of the categories below, mark an X at the point that best reflects your position or tendency. Be as honest and objective as possible. In the notes section, explain why you positioned yourself where you did. Are you far left or right or somewhere in the middle?

Your Christian Witness

Always speak the truth, no matter the effects	Mostly speak the truth	Consistently speak the truth with love	Mostly speak with love	Always speak with love, despite the truth

Notes: _____

_____

_____

_____

Your Ministry

Focused only on evangelism and teaching	Focused mostly on evangelism and teaching	Focused equally on both	Focused mostly on compassion-ate ministry	Focused only on com-passionate ministry

Notes: _____

_____

_____

_____

Your Understanding of God's Character

Only loving, compassion-ate, gracious	Mostly loving, compassion-ate, gracious	Equally both	Mostly righ-teous, just, wrathful	Only righ-teous, just, wrathful

Notes: _____

_____

_____

_____

Your Lifestyle

Focused only on faith or belief	Focused mostly on faith or belief	Focused equally on faith and good work	Focused mostly on good works	Focused only on good works

Notes: _____

_____

_____

_____

_____

2. Did any of these assessments raise questions for you? If so, write them below. Discuss these questions with your group, or spend time exploring them this week.

    _____

    _____

    _____

    _____

    _____

3. What is your overall opinion of keeping Christian life and belief in wholistic balance? Write a one- or two-sentence statement below.

    _____

    _____

    _____

    _____

The next session: *analyzing the divided mind and life*

～ The Divided Mind and Life

The Memorial to the German Resistance in Berlin spotlights the courageous efforts of Germans who sacrificed their lives to stand against one of the most evil regimes in human history. The museum also displays disturbing photographs. Pictures of Protestant pastors and Catholic priests giving the Nazi salute. Pictures of swastika banners adorning Christian churches—swastika banners with Christ's cross in the center.

The distressing reality is that many churches during the Nazi era in Germany fell silent in the face of radical evil or openly supported Adolf Hitler's regime. During Hitler's rise to power, 95 percent of all Germans claimed to be Christian.[1] One-third were Catholic and two-thirds were Protestant.[2] How could so many followers of the Prince of Peace support such a wicked government, or stand idly by while it slaughtered millions of Jews?

While there are no simple answers to this question, a possible cause can be traced to the rule of the German chancellor Otto von Bismarck (1815–1898). According to author and pastor Erwin Lutzer, "Bismarck claimed to have had a conversion experience to Christianity . . . but he was faced with the realization that as a [politician] he had to violate the moral principles that governed his private behavior as a Christian. He reasoned that when acting as a servant of the state, a man was not bound by the same morality he should have as an individual." In short, Bismarck believed there "must be a split between private and public morality."[3]

This double standard became known as the doctrine of the two spheres. According to this doctrine, spiritual issues such as salvation and eternal life extend from the sphere governed by the church and scripture. Everything else, and especially "worldly" matters such as politics, law, and diplomacy, exist in a separate sphere where biblical principles do not apply. This divided mindset gained widespread acceptance among German Christians in the years preceding Hitler's rise to power. According to the two-spheres mentality, "Christ is Lord of the church, but the King (or Fuehrer) is, in a manner of speaking, lord over the political sphere, and the private values of honesty . . . and compassion were not translated into public values."[4]

Ironically, during this same period a spiritual renewal movement swept through the Lutheran church. A movement "that advocated a return to biblical [faithfulness], the worship of God . . . and personal devotion to Christ."[5] Yet because of the two-spheres mentality rooted in the German church, the movement stressed evangelism and preaching Christ but withdrew from the intellectual debates raging across Germany. Because of the church's divided mindset, "this renewal movement had [little] influence on stemming the Nazi tide."[6]

When Adolf Hitler attained supreme power, the two-spheres mentality was pushed to its limit. Ultimately, Nazism forced German Christians to "choose between a Christ who was Lord over a shrinking 'spiritual sphere' and Christ who was Lord over all."[7]

Hitler had no intention of sharing power with Christian leaders. He would not allow the cross of Christ and the broken cross of the Nazi swastika to coexist. On January 4, 1934, the Nazi government issued a decree known as the Muzzling Order, which forbade German clergy to speak about social or political controversy in sermons.[8] The Muzzling Order rocked the German church. Could a pastor be faithful simply by preaching Christ crucified, or were there implications of this message that had to be lived out, even if authorities considered such actions controversial?[9]

Many pastors defied the Muzzling Order, and as a result the German Evangelical Church divided. Those who defied the order became known as the Confessing Church. One of its key leaders, Karl Barth, powerfully proclaimed, "We reject the false doctrine that there are realms of our life in which we belong not to Jesus Christ, but to other masters, realms where we do not need to be justified and sanctified by him."[10] The leaders of the Confessing Church, which included Dietrich Bonhoeffer, believed that the two-spheres doctrine was a lie. They concluded that committed Christians needed to live their faith in every area of life."[11] For taking this stand, many of them paid the ultimate price: death in the Nazi camps.

Throughout history Christians have created distinctions between a spiritual realm that honors Jesus as Lord and a secular realm that does not. While our lives contain many parts, the Bible specifies that Jesus should be Lord over every part (1 Cor. 10:31). As Christians we desire to place everything under his authority. The divided mindset and life, like that within part of the German church during the Nazi era, remains a serious problem for Christians around the world today.

In this session we'll explore the roots and consequences of this divided mindset and how it threatens the concept of biblical discipleship.

KEY WORDS TO KNOW
The Cost of Discipleship

Discipleship

The root word *disciple* derives from the Latin word *discipulus*, which means pupil or learner. In the Gospels, Christ's followers, especially the twelve apostles, were known as disciples. The disciples' bond to Jesus extended beyond a simple student-teacher relationship. Discipleship to the Master required personal allegiance and complete loyalty. They put him first and applied his teaching to every area of life, regardless of the personal cost. *Discipleship* refers to the learning and growing process of becoming more like Jesus, in both how we think and how we behave.

Compartmentalize

To compartmentalize is to separate something that is "whole" into isolated compartments or categories. Compartmentalization in life is the opposite of wholism and works against biblical teachings.

KEY VERSES TO READ
Bringing Every Thought Captive

> We demolish arguments and every pretension that sets itself up against the knowledge of God, and we take captive every thought to make it obedient to Christ.
>
> —*2 Corinthians 10:5*

1. What is the imagery that the apostle Paul uses in this verse? Why would he choose such strong language?

   _____

   _____

   _____

2. What are we to "take captive," and why are we to do this?

   _____

   _____

3. Does this verse apply only to spiritual or religious topics? Explain your answer.

   _____

   _____

   _____

4. What can we do to "take captive every thought"? See 2 Timothy 3:16–17.

   _____

   _____

   _____

BIBLICAL INSIGHTS
Dangerously Divided Minds

The New Testament presents discipleship as all-inclusive. Because Christ is the creator, sustainer, and ruler of all things, his lordship impacts every area of our lives. If we have a divided mindset and do not actively allow Christ to rule certain parts of our lives, we are allowing another lord—whoever or whatever it may be—to control us. For this reason the apostle Paul tells us to "take captive every thought and make it obedient to Christ." Elsewhere Paul says, "Whatever you do, do it all for the glory of God" (1 Cor. 10:31). Our call as disciples is to live to the glory of God according to the principles and truths of Scripture. Discipleship extends to all aspects of our lives, including our families, vocations, studies, leisure activities, and daily routines. It also applies to our many roles—as parents, siblings, children, employees, supervisors, students, teachers, leaders, and followers.

As we train our minds to seek wholistic, biblical discipleship, the many parts of our lives will join together to honor God. Our lives will reflect the wholeness and integrity that we were created to possess.

Errors in the East and West

Thinking and living wholistically does not come naturally to people, whether they are from Eastern or Western cultures. Many Eastern cultures emphasize the whole at the expense of the parts. This is reflected in belief systems such as pantheism, where ultimate reality is one substance—an infinite, impersonal force. Everything else that appears to exist is an illusion. This belief manifests in the social arena where the group (the whole) is considered more important than the individuals (the parts). In Japan, for example, a popular cultural proverb is "The nail that sticks up gets hammered down." There is little respect for individuality. The group is all-important.

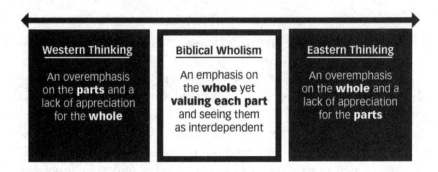

In contrast, Western cultures focus less on the whole and more on indi-viduals, emphasizing individual rights and individual choice. When radical individualism prevails, when a person has no regard for others, commu-nity life suffers. For many people around the world, thinking wholistically requires retraining the mind.

The Divided Mindset in Everyday Life

If our natural tendency is to emphasize parts and lose sight of the whole, our lives will be marked by compartmentalization. The time we spend in various activities—with family, at work, at church, at play—will reside in separate compartments in our minds with little interaction between them. If I am a Christian and think this way, I face the danger of putting my faith into a box marked "Private Beliefs" and treating them as personal, while adopting whatever views are current in my professional or social circles. Author and scholar Nancy Pearcey writes, "We probably all know of Christian teachers who uncritically accept the latest secular theories of education; Christian businessmen who run their operations by accepted secular management theories; Christian ministries that mirror the com-mercial world's marketing techniques. . . . While sincere in their faith, they have absorbed their views on just about everything else by osmosis from the surrounding culture."[12]

Christian businessman John Beckett was such a person. For John, "Sundays were Sundays, with the rest of the week largely detached, operat-ing by a different set of rules."[13] In his book *Loving Monday* he tells how he struggled to overcome this compartmentalized thinking. Having accepted Christ as an adult, Beckett soon discovered "a wide gulf" between his new faith and his work life: "I found myself living in two separate worlds." He felt that it was "impossible to serve God by being a man or woman in business. . . . For years, I thought my involvement in business was a second-class endeavor—necessary to put bread on the table, but somehow less noble than more sacred pursuits like being a minister or a missionary."[14]

Compartmentalization in Culture

Today in many Western countries, it is considered normal and even good to live compartmentalized lives. Many believe that what they do in their private lives should have no impact on their public lives and how they conduct themselves in public. In the religious sphere in the United States, this outlook is encouraged by the notion of "separation of the church and state," which is understood by many to mean the elimination of Christian beliefs and practices from the public sphere. You are free to practice your faith in your private life (in your home or in church), but it is inappropriate to be a Christian in public. Today, many Christians inadvertently go along with this distortion. What was originally intended to prevent the imposition of a state church or religion by the government has now become a call to ban Christianity from public life altogether. Yet as the Confessing Church in Germany discovered during the Nazi era, God cannot be tucked neatly away in a box labeled "Private Beliefs." Christ demands to be Lord of all. There can be no middle ground. He never intended there to be.[15]

DISCOVERY QUESTIONS
A Call to Comprehensive Discipleship

Discipleship to Christ requires submission and obedience. A divided mind and compartmentalized life contradicts Christ's call to commitment. Open your Bible and read afresh what Jesus and the apostles say about discipleship.

1. Read Mark 1:16–18. What is the starting point for all disciples of Jesus?

   _____

   _____

   _____

2. What does Jesus' call to "follow me" imply for his disciples? See Mark 10:28.

   _____

   _____

   _____

3. Read Matthew 28:18 and Colossians 1:15–18. Why does Jesus deserve our allegiance and submission?

   _____

   _____

   _____

4. Read Philippians 3:4b–14. What did Paul give up to gain Christ? In comparison to knowing and gaining Christ, how does Paul describe the things he gave up?

   _____

   _____

   _____

5. Read Mark 8:34. What does being a disciple of Christ involve? In your own words, describe what Jesus means when he says, "He must deny himself and take up his cross."

   _____

   _____

   _____

6. According to Mark 8:35, how do we "save" our lives—or "have [life] to the full," as the apostle John says in John 10:10?

_____

_____

_____

7.   Read Mark 10:17–23. What did the rich young man desire in verse 17? In verse 21, what instructions did Jesus give? Was the young man willing to pay the price to gain his desire?

_____

_____

_____

8.   Why is it so difficult for those who are rich to follow Jesus? See Matthew 6:24.

_____

_____

_____

KEY POINTS TO REMEMBER
The Perils of Divided Lives

1.   Thinking wholistically is rarely easy or natural. It often requires us to intentionally change the way we think.
2.   Traditionally, people raised in the East emphasize the whole at the expense of the parts, and people raised in the West emphasize the parts at the expense of the whole. Both of these viewpoints are contrary to a biblical worldview.
3.   If we emphasize the parts at the expense of the whole, it usually leads to a compartmentalized lifestyle, with little or no interaction among the parts.
4.   God cannot be tucked neatly into a box labeled "Private Beliefs." Jesus demands to be Lord of all.

CLOSING THOUGHTS
Every Area, Every Part

Christ's call to follow him is comprehensive and demands our entire lives—every area and every part. One of Satan's great deceptions is that a life of fully committed discipleship is a life of drudgery, sorrow, and sacrifice. What you need to do, Satan seems to say, is take control of your own life. You know better than God how to realize your dreams for happiness and significance. When followers of Christ fall for this deception, they put God in a box. "He can be Lord over some parts of my life, but I'll control the rest!" For other Christians, life is divided into "spiritual" and "secular" categories. The spiritual category has to do with personal beliefs, church attendance, and prayer life. The secular category comprises the rest of life, including work, education, and recreation. Both cases lead to divided minds and divided lives that lack integrity and fall short of the vision of discipleship put forward by Christ and the apostles. But as we allow God to be Lord over all of our lives and seek to honor him through everything we do, we gain what the apostle John describes as "life to the full" (John 10:10).

When author John Beckett finally overcame the sacred-secular split, for the first time he was able to regard his work "as having great worth to God." As "a business person, I was no longer a second-class citizen. . . . Nor did I need to leave my Christian convictions and biblical values outside the office entrance when I headed into work on Monday morning."[16] This same liberating experience can be ours if we put aside our divided minds and embrace a wholistic life.

PERSONAL APPLICATION
Giving It All to God

Becoming a disciple of Jesus begins with the intentional decision to do so. It doesn't just happen. Maybe you have never intentionally decided to follow Christ with everything you are, with everything you have, and in everything you do. Or maybe you want to renew a vow you made in the past. Here are some suggestions for taking the next step:

1. Select a time when you can get away by yourself to a quiet place where you will not be distracted. Block out no less than two hours so you don't feel rushed. Mark the date and time on your calendar and commit to it.
2. Make this a solemn occasion. Come before the Lord with humility and confess those areas of your life that you have not surrendered to him. Be specific and honest about how you have not followed him with your whole life.
3. Carefully consider what changes you will need to make to follow Jesus with your whole life. What habits or practices are not compatible with following Jesus? What priorities need to change? Write these things down and pray about them.
4. After counting the cost of discipleship, make a firm decision. Ask God to give you strength through his Holy Spirit.
5. Let those around you, such as your close friends and family members, know about your decision to follow Christ.

The next session: *what it means to live a life of wholism*

⬱ Living with Wholism in Mind

In the previous session we examined the destructive consequences of compartmentalized minds and lives. Many
Christians today live in two worlds—the "spiritual" world of faith and
church and the "secular" world of work and daily life. In so dividing their
lives, they reduce Christianity to a series of religious meetings and church-
based programs. Their Christian faith is privately engaging but irrelevant
to their social, economic, or political concerns. This sacred-secular divide
is so common that when we witness a life that is undivided and totally
devoted to Christ, we take notice. Such a life was lived by the nineteenth-
century Dutchman Abraham Kuyper.

The son of a minister, Kuyper was born on October 29, 1837. At age
twenty-one he followed in his father's footsteps by attending seminary,
earning a doctorate of theology on September 20, 1862. The summer after
his graduation, he married Johanna Schaay, and the young couple soon
moved to the town of Beesd, where Kuyper served as the pastor of the
town's small church. Several members of the Beesd congregation were
committed Christians who confronted Kuyper on unbiblical doctrines he
had acquired at the theologically liberal seminary he had attended. They

also questioned him about whether he truly had a saving faith in Christ. God used these loving, persistent church members to lead their pastor back to the simple truths of Scripture and faith in Christ.[1]

As a devoted Christian, Kuyper sought to bring God's truth into all areas of his life and into everything he did—and he did a great deal! He was a politician and statesman. He served as a member of Parliament and was prime minister of the Netherlands from 1901 to 1905. He was a national church leader, theologian, and pastor. He was a key developer of the idea we now call "worldview." He was an educator and the founder of a major university, the Free University in Amsterdam, which today has over fourteen thousand students. He was a journalist and writer who edited two daily newspapers, *The Herald* and *The Standard,* until the age of 82. He was a devoted husband and father of two daughters and five sons. His Christian faith infused all areas of his life. It provided continuity, integrity, and dynamism into everything he did. Abraham Kuyper was a man who lived with wholism in mind.

What drove Kuyper? He passionately pursued a life totally committed to the lordship of Jesus Christ in all things. "One desire has been the ruling passion of my life," said Kuyper, "that in spite of all worldly opposition, God's holy ordinances shall be established again in the home, in the school and in the state for the good of the people . . . until the nation pays homage again to God."[2]

For Kuyper, the lordship of Jesus extended "from theology to the arts, from politics to science, from individuals to entire institutions. Serving Jesus necessarily entailed submission to his Lordship in all areas of human thought and activity."[3] Kuyper saw Christianity as a total world and life view, not merely a spiritual or theological system. One of his most famous quotes reflects this thoroughly Christ-centered belief system: "There is not a square inch of the universe over which King Jesus does not claim, 'Mine!'"[4] It was this conviction that led Kuyper from the pastorate into writing, politics, and education. In each of these areas he based his activity on God's revealed Word and was dedicated to discovering and applying biblical principles that underlay them. "God's majesty and sovereignty require that we believe God's Word," he proclaimed, "not because of what it says, but because it is his Word, not because we think it beautiful and true, but because he has spoken it."[5]

KEY WORDS TO KNOW
Living a Life of Integrity

Dichotomy

Dichotomy refers to the division of something into two or more mutually exclusive categories. In this session, this word is used to describe a lifestyle in which the various parts of life (family life, work, faith, etc.) are separated into mutually exclusive categories. This is a *dichotomized* life and is the opposite of a wholistic lifestyle.

Integrate

To integrate is to coordinate, or blend two or more things into a whole.

Integrity

Integrity means a state of being whole or undivided. Its root word is *integrate*, which is derived from *integer*, "a complete entity." Integrity is often used to describe a quality of character marked by honesty and incorruptibility. In this session, we describe a life of wholism as a life of integrity.

Submission

The root word *submit* means to yield to governance or authority. Submission is the act of yielding to an authority. As Christians, our ultimate authority is God and his revealed will or intentions in Scripture. Jesus' life is our model of submission. He said, "I do exactly what my Father has commanded me" (John 14:31).

KEY VERSES TO READ
All for God

So whether you eat or drink or whatever you do, do it all for the glory of God.

—1 Corinthians 10:31

> And whatever you do, whether in word or deed, do it all
> in the name of the Lord Jesus, giving thanks to God the
> Father through him.
>
> *—Colossians 3:17*

1. What are the similarities and differences between these two verses?

    _____

    _____

    _____

2. What are we to do for the glory of God? What are we to do in the name of the Lord Jesus?

    _____

    _____

3. How do the examples of "eating and drinking" strengthen Paul's point in 1 Corinthians 10:31?

    _____

    _____

4. Read 1 Corinthians 10:23–31. In verse 26 Paul quotes from Psalm 24:1: "The earth is the Lord's, and everything in it." How does this verse highlight what Paul is admonishing in verse 31?

    _____

    _____

    _____

BIBLICAL INSIGHTS

Doing Everything to the Glory of God

In the introduction to this session we said that Abraham Kuyper lived with wholism in mind. What does that mean? First, let's refresh our thinking on the definition of wholism.

Wholism is the idea that the parts must be understood in relationship to the whole. To see something *wholistically* is to see both its whole and the interdependence of its parts. We can apply this concept to how we live. Our lives have many parts. Consider how you spend your time during the course of a typical day or week. What are the various roles you play? What are the different tasks you carry out? Your roles may include being a husband or wife, father or mother, boss or employee, subordinate, leader, church member, and citizen. Your day may be divided between time at work, time with family, time at church, time driving to and from various activities, and some personal time spent resting, reading, eating and drinking, or exercising. All of these roles and tasks represent different parts of life. Wholism is seeing the connection between these various parts and roles. It is seeing the greater whole of your life that holds the parts together and gives them meaning and purpose.

As followers of Jesus, we acknowledge that Jesus is Lord over all. If he is Lord over all, he is to be Lord over every part of our lives. As Colossians 1:18 states, he is to have "supremacy" in "everything." This is why the apostle Paul exhorts us to "do [everything] for the glory of God" (1 Cor. 10:31) and to "do [everything] in the name of the Lord Jesus" (Col. 3:17). This is the greater "whole" that is to bring unity to our lives. A wholistic life is one lived in complete submission to God, not just in "spiritual" things, but in everything. If my commitment to the Lord Jesus exists at the very center of everything I do, my life has integrity. My faith unites the parts of my life into a greater whole, with all the parts giving glory to God. Jesus lived such a life, and his life has been the prime example for people throughout history, including Abraham Kuyper. God desires all of us to live lives of wholism and integrity.

Integrating Faith and Vocation

The idea of living wholistically may be easier to understand than it is to live out. We can fall into the trap of compartmentalizing our lives and applying the wisdom and principles contained in the Bible to some parts of our lives but not others.

One part that often gets separated from our faith is our work or vocation. This is a problem that has plagued the church for centuries. Prior to the Reformation, the Catholic Church viewed the work of lay people as inferior to the work of priests, nuns, or monks. Martin Luther directly confronted this belief in his tract "The Babylonian Captivity of the Church."

> The work of monks and priests, however holy and arduous they be, do not differ one whit in the sight of God from the works of the rustic laborer in the field or the woman going about her household tasks. . . . All work [should be] measured before God by faith alone. . . . Indeed, the menial housework of a manservant or maidservant is often more acceptable to God than all the fastings and other works of a monk or priest, because the monk or priest lacks faith.[6]

According to Luther, if we do our work in the light of our faith and to the glory of God, we are not to view it as something less spiritual than the work of pastors, priests, or other religious workers. God is the Lord of all of life. He is the Lord of personal devotion, church life, and missions, *and* he is the Lord of business, arts, and science. So long as our work is morally acceptable to God, it is to be done in faith and to the glory of God.

The Bible is instructive for more than "spiritual" topics like redemption and eternal life; its wisdom and principles apply to all areas of life, including how we think about and carry out the work we do. For example, if you are a Christian farmer, the Bible provides the conceptual framework from which you should practice farming: God, the creator of the physical universe, gave humans dominion over the earth and the task of caring for his creation (Gen. 1). From Scripture we learn godly principles of earth-keeping and stewardship, which directly relate to farming. And the same applies to other vocational areas, including business, government, health-care, the arts, and education.

From this perspective, our work is a primary means *through* which (not merely *in* which) we serve Christ and advance his kingdom. According to pastor Grover Gunn, "Every valid occupation offers special opportunities to submit to God. The Christian legislator can acknowledge God's law as the highest law. The Christian educator can teach that all the treasures of wisdom and knowledge are hidden in Christ. The Christian businessperson can conduct business with honesty and integrity. The Christian doctor can respect the sanctity of human life. The Christian farmer can treat God's earth respectfully while working to produce a bounty."[7] Furthermore, because Jesus is our ultimate "boss," we are to do our work *for him*—with excellence and in a manner pleasing to him. "Whatever you do, work at it with all your heart, as working for the Lord, not for men, since you know that you will receive an inheritance from the Lord as a reward. It is the Lord Christ you are serving" (Col. 3:23–24). Our work is important to God, if for nothing else, because we spend so much of our waking hours doing it! Perhaps the greatest single statement that we will ever make in our lives for the cause of Christ—for good or bad—is how we do our work.

Integrating Faith and Family

Another part of life that is often separated from faith and service to the Lord is how we interact with our families. Yet if we strive to live wholistically, we will ask, How can I glorify God through my family life? How can I glorify God as a parent, spouse, sibling, or child? How can my family bring glory to God? Rather than taking our cues from our surrounding culture, we must go to the Bible to see how God designed families to function.

The Bible provides specific instruction on how we ought to function as families to the glory of God (see Deut. 11:18–21; Prov. 13:24; Eph. 5:22–6:4; 1 Pet. 3:1–7). We bring glory to God as we obey his commands in the area of family life. And when we obey, not only does the kingdom of God advance within our own families, but also our families become a powerful tool in God's hands for advancing his kingdom in our communities and nations. Pastor Gunn states that our family provides us with

> our first and primary opportunity to submit to God's . . . authority. The husband should lead his wife with sacrificial love and the wife should submit to her husband with respectful obedience. Parents should provide for their

children the liberating structure of discipline and children should honor and obey their parents. . . . The family should be the microcosmic kingdom, where the Godly father proclaims, "as for me and my house, we will serve the Lord" (Josh. 24:15).[8]

Integrating Faith and Everything!

When we seek to glorify God in all areas of our lives, even in simple everyday tasks like eating and drinking, our entire lives are filled with purpose and dynamism. Even menial tasks are filled with new importance and dignity. Our lives are no longer divided into "spiritual" and "secular" activities. Instead, God's truth is infused into every area of life.

The sixteenth century European Reformers used a simple Latin phrase to capture this important perspective: *coram Deo,* which means "before the face of God." For the Christians of that generation, each moment and each task was lived before the face of God, under the authority of God, and to the glory of God. They understood that Jesus had a right to their full devotion, whether they were worshiping in church, cooking a meal, plowing a field, practicing law, preaching the gospel, or feeding the hungry. Os Guinness writes, "Luther declared that God and the angels smile when a man changes a diaper. William Tyndale wrote that, if our desire is to please God, pouring water, washing dishes, cobbling shoes, and preaching the Word 'is all one.' William Perkins claimed polishing shoes was a sanctified and holy act. Bishop Thomas Becon wrote, 'Our Savior Christ was a carpenter. His apostles were fishermen. St. Paul was a tent-maker.'"[9] When a person lives with wholism in mind—when Jesus is made Lord of every part of life—then even everyday work is given dignity and significance.

DISCOVERY QUESTIONS
Submitting to Christ's Lordship

Central to living a life of wholism is submitting joyfully to the lordship of Christ. Open your Bible to read more about Christ's all-encompassing reign over everything—including your life.

1. Begin by reading Psalm 24:1. What does this verse reveal about God and about his creation?

    _____

    _____

    _____

2. Read Isaiah 6:1–3. Describe Isaiah's vision. What does this vision reveal about God and about the earth?

    _____

    _____

    _____

3. Read Daniel 4:34–35. Describe King Nebuchadnezzar's conclusions about God.

    _____

    _____

    _____

    _____

4. Read Matthew 28:18. Over what and whom does Jesus exercise authority? Does he exercise his authority presently?

    _____

    _____

    _____

5. The New Testament is clear that Jesus is king over all creation, not just in the future when he returns, but today as well. Yet we live in a broken world where many do not acknowledge his lordship and authority. How does Jesus' parable of the wheat and the weeds in Matthew 13:24–29, 36–40 help us understand this?

    _____

    _____

    _____

    _____

6. Read 1 Corinthians 6:19–20. Who "purchased" us?

   _____

   _____

7. Read John 3:16 and 1 Peter 1:18–19. What was the price that God and Jesus paid to purchase us?

   _____

   _____

   _____

8. Read Romans 12:1. What should our response be to him who sacrificed himself for us? In your own words, describe what it mean to be a "living sacrifice."

   _____

   _____

   _____

   _____

9. Read John 14:31. Describe the relationship between Jesus and the Father. Would you characterize your relationship to God in these same terms? Why or why not?

   _____

   _____

   _____

   _____

KEY POINTS TO REMEMBER
A Life of Wholism in Review

1. A life of wholism entails seeing the parts of life and our roles in light of a greater whole. As Christians, our devotion to Jesus provides this greater whole. When we live in light of Jesus' lordship, our lives reflect integrity or wholeness.

2. One of the most important parts of life is work or vocation. When Jesus is seen as lord over our vocations, they become a primary means through which we serve Christ. Every valid occupation offers special opportunities to submit to God and advance his kingdom.

3. Another important part of life is family life. The Bible provides us with the principles to function as families that bring glory to God. Through obedience to God, families can advance God's kingdom in their communities and nations.

4. When we live a life of wholism, everything we do is filled with importance and dignity. Even simple everyday tasks, when done in faith, take on a fresh sense of purpose and dynamism.

CLOSING THOUGHTS
Living the Adventure

God is the Maker of the universe and everything in it. As his creatures we are to live in one inclusive world, not a world divided between "spiritual" and "secular" realms, where faith applies or doesn't apply. We are to live under the lordship of Christ. We are to live *coram Deo*, before the face of God. E. Stanley Jones (1884–1973), missionary-statesman to India, wrote powerfully of how exciting life can be when it is lived to the fullest for Christ and his kingdom. The person who lives *coram Deo*, he said,

> sees God . . . working with him and in him and backing him. He sees God at work everywhere. The universe becomes alive with God—every bush aflame with him, every event full of destiny, life an exciting adventure with God. You see him at work in you, in events, in the universe. He talks with you, guides you. You work in the same business, in the same occupation—the Kingdom. And it is the most thrilling, exciting business and occupation in the world. All else is tame and . . . dull. Here you are working at the biggest job, on the biggest scale, at the most

worthwhile task, at the greatest outcome—the kingdom of God on earth.[10]

Dallas Willard describes it this way: "Jesus came among us to show and teach the life for which we were made. . . . By relying on his word and presence we are enabled to reintegrate the little realm that makes up our life into the infinite rule of God. . . . Caught up in his active rule, our deeds become an element in God's eternal history."[11]

PERSONAL APPLICATION
I Surrender All

For followers of Christ, there can be nothing more important than the integrity of living our whole lives in accordance with God's revealed truth. Use the questions below to help you apply this session's principles to your life.

1. Which statement below best describes your current relationship with Christ?
    ◆   I trust Jesus only as my Savior. I make decisions based on what I think is best, apart from my personal religious beliefs.
    ◆   I trust Jesus as my Savior and partially as my Lord. I have given him control and authority over some areas of my life, but I have control over other areas.
    ◆   I trust Jesus as both my Savior and my Lord. I seek to live in total devotion to him and submit to his will in all areas of my life.

2. Take time to consider which areas of your life you easily give over to Christ's lordship and which areas you don't. What is preventing you from releasing certain areas to him? Pray and ask God to help you release these areas into his control. Consider sharing this with a believer whom you trust and ask him or her to pray for you.

_____

_____

_____

_____

_____

_____

3. Life decisions provide us with opportunities to reflect on the degree
    to which Jesus is Lord of our lives. Think about important life deci-
    sions you have made. In what ways did your relationship with Jesus
    influence the decision-making process? What possible decisions lie in
    your future? How can you honor Jesus as Lord and Master as you face
    them?

_____

_____

_____

_____

_____

_____

4. Not only should our faith in Jesus influence major turning points in
    our lives, but it should influence each and every task we engage in, no
    matter how small or seemingly inconsequential. Think of the mun-
    dane, everyday tasks that you do regularly. In what ways do you do
    these tasks to the glory of God?

_____

_____

_____

_____

_____

_____

The next session: *understanding wholistic ministry*

⮌ Wholistic Ministry

When Englishman William Carey (1761–1834) arrived in India in 1793, it marked a major milestone in the history of Christian missions and in the history of India. Carey established the Serampore Mission—the first modern Protestant mission in the non-English-speaking world—near Calcutta on January 10, 1800.[1] From this base, he labored for over three decades to spread the gospel throughout the land. In the end his triumph was spectacular. Through his unfailing love for the people of India and his relentless campaign against "the spiritual forces of evil" (Eph. 6:12), India was transformed. Asian historian Hugh Tinker summarizes Carey's impact on India this way: "And so in Serampore, on the banks of the river Hooghly, the principle elements of modern South Asia—the press, the university, social consciousness—all came to light."[2]

Who was William Carey? He was exactly the kind of man that the Lord seems to delight in using to accomplish great things; in other words, the kind of person that most of us would least expect. He was raised in a small, rural English town where he received little formal education. His chief source of income came through his work as a cobbler (a shoemaker).

He had an awkward, homely appearance, having lost almost all his hair in childhood. Upon his arrival in India and throughout his years there, he was harassed by British colonists, deserted by his mission-sending agency, and opposed by younger missionary recruits who were sent to help him. Despite these setbacks, Carey became perhaps the most influential person in the largest outpost of the British Empire.[3]

Carey didn't go to India merely to start new churches or set up medical clinics for the poor. He was driven by a more comprehensive vision—a vision for discipling the nation. "Carey saw India not as a foreign country to be exploited, but as his heavenly Father's land to be loved and served, a society where truth, not ignorance, needed to rule."[4] He looked outward across the land and asked himself, "If Jesus were the Lord of India, what would it look like? What would be different?" This question set his agenda and led to his involvement in a remarkable variety of activities aimed at glorifying God and advancing his kingdom. Following are highlights of Carey's work described in Vishal and Ruth Mangalwadi's outstanding book *The Legacy of William Carey: A Model for the Transformation of a Culture.*[5]

Carey was horrified that India, one of the most fertile countries in the world, had been allowed to become an uncultivated jungle abandoned to wild beasts and serpents. Therefore he carried out a systematic survey of agriculture and campaigned for agriculture reform. He introduced the Linnean system of gardening and published the first science texts in India. He did this because he believed that nature is declared "good" by its Creator; it is not *maya* (illusion) to be shunned, as Hindus believe, but a subject worthy of human study.

Carey introduced the idea of savings banks to India to fight the all-pervasive social evil of usury (the lending of money at excessive interest). He believed that God, being righteous, hated this practice which made investment, industry, commerce, and economic development impossible.

Believing that Jesus' love extended to leprosy patients, Carey was the first to campaign for humane treatment of India's leprosy victims. Before then, lepers were often buried or burned alive because of the belief that a violent death purified the body on its way to reincarnation into a new healthy existence.

Carey also established the first newspaper ever printed in an Asian language because he believed that "above all forms of truth and faith, Christianity seeks free discussion." His English-language journal, *Friend of India*, was the force that gave birth to the social-reform movement in India in the first half of the nineteenth century.

Soon Carey had translated the Bible into over forty different Indian languages. He transformed the Bengali language, previously considered "fit for only demons and women," into the foremost literary language of India. He wrote gospel ballads in Bengali to bring the Hindu love of music to the service of his Lord.

He began dozens of schools for Indian children of all castes and launched the first college in Asia. He desired to develop the Indian mind and liberate it from darkness and superstition.

He was the first man to stand against the ruthless murders and widespread oppression of women. Women in India were being crushed through polygamy, female infanticide, child marriage, widow burning, euthanasia, and forced illiteracy—all sanctioned by religion. Carey opened schools for girls. When widows converted to Christianity, he arranged marriages for them. It was his persistent, twenty-five-year battle against widow burning (known as *sati*) that finally led to the formal banning of this horrible religious practice.

William Carey was a pioneer of the modern Christian missionary movement, a movement that has since reached every corner of the world. Although a man of simple origins, he used his God-given genius and every available means to serve his Creator and illumine the dark corners of India with the light of the truth. Carey was a pioneer of modern wholistic ministry.

KEY WORDS TO KNOW

The Meaning of Ministry

Ministry

In the New Testament the Greek word for ministry is *diakonein*. It was used to describe the humble, loving service of Christians to humanity at large and to fellow Christians. Ministry is divine resources meeting human needs through loving channels to the glory of God.

Substantial

In this session *substantial* describes something that is mostly, but not fully, complete. For example, a person's eyewitness account of an event may be substantially accurate or complete; however, it is possible that he or she missed minor details. The kingdom of God brings substantial healing to our fallen world; that is, it brings real, significant healing, yet healing that will remain partial and incomplete until Christ's return.

KEY VERSE TO READ

Teaching, Preaching, and Healing

> Jesus went throughout Galilee, teaching in their synagogues, preaching the good news of the kingdom, and healing every disease and sickness among the people.
> —*Matthew 4:23*

1. Matthew 4:23 provides a concise description of Jesus' ministry. What are the three parts of Jesus' ministry highlighted in this verse?

   _____

   _____

2. What is the *whole* ministry of Jesus, to which each part contributes? See Matthew 6:9–10.

   _____

   _____

3. Consider the relationship between the three parts and the whole of Jesus' ministry. Is any part unnecessary in accomplishing the whole? What would be the result of removing a part?

   _____

   _____

BIBLICAL INSIGHTS
God's Big Agenda

William Carey's ministry in India was wholistic. For something to be wholistic, it must have multiple parts that contribute to a greater whole. What is the "whole" that all Christian ministry activities contribute to? Through an examination of Christ's earthly ministry, we see that the "whole" is glorifying God and advancing his kingdom through the discipling of nations (Matt. 24:14; 28:18–20). This is God's "big agenda"—the principal task that he works through his church to accomplish.

If this is the whole, then what are the parts? The Key Verse from the previous page, Matthew 4:23, highlights three parts: preaching, teaching, and healing. Because these three parts are essential to the whole, let's look at each one more carefully.

Preaching entails proclaiming the gospel—God's gracious invitation for people everywhere to live in his kingdom, have their sins forgiven, be spiritually reborn, and become children of God through faith in Christ. Proclaiming the gospel is essential to wholistic ministry, for unless lost and broken people are spiritually reborn into a living relationship with God—unless they become "a new creation" (2 Cor. 5:17)—all efforts to bring hope, healing, and transformation are doomed to fail. People everywhere need their relationship with God restored.

Teaching entails instructing people in the foundational truths of Scripture. It is associated with discipleship—helping people to live in obedience to God and his Word in every area of life. In Matthew 28:20 Jesus tells his disciples to "teach [the nations] to obey everything I have commanded you." Unless believers are taught to *obey* Christ's commands, their growth may be hindered. Colossians 3:16 says, "Let the word of Christ dwell in you richly as you teach and admonish one another with all wisdom."

Healing involves the tangible demonstrations of the present reality of the kingdom in the midst of our hurting and broken world. When Jesus came, he demonstrated the present reality of God's kingdom by healing people. "The blind receive sight, the lame walk, those who have leprosy are cured, the deaf hear, the dead are raised, and the good news is preached to the poor," was Jesus' report to his cousin John the Baptist in Matthew 11:4–5. Jesus didn't just preach the good news; he demonstrated it by healing all forms of brokenness. Unless ministry to people's physical needs accompanies evangelism and discipleship, our message will be empty, weak, and irrelevant. This is particularly true where poverty is rampant. The apostle John admonishes, "If anyone has material possessions and sees his brother in need but has no pity on him, how can the love of God be in him? Dear children, let us not love with words or tongue but with actions and in truth" (1 John 3:17–18).

Here's a picture of the basic elements of a biblically balanced, wholistic ministry:

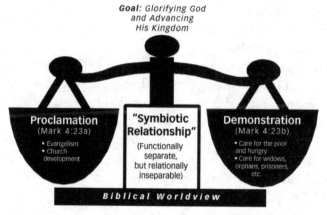

First, there are multiple parts—preaching, teaching, and healing. These parts have distinct functions, yet they are inseparable. All are essential in contributing to the whole, which is glorifying God and advancing his kingdom. Lastly, each part rests on the solid foundation of the biblical worldview. In other words, each is understood and implemented through the basic premises of Scripture. In summary, preaching, teaching, and healing are three indispensable parts of wholistic ministry, whose purpose is to advance God's kingdom "on earth as it is in heaven" (Matt. 6:10). Without these parts working together seamlessly, our ministry is less than what Christ intends, and will lack power to transform lives and nations.

Broken Relationships

To comprehend the nature and purpose of wholistic ministry, two concepts must be understood. First is the comprehensive impact of humanity's spiritual rebellion. Second is that our loving, compassionate God is presently unfolding his plan to redeem and restore all things broken through the Fall.

When Adam and Eve turned their backs on God in the Garden of Eden (Gen. 3:1–6), the consequences of their sin were devastating and far reaching; they affected the very order of the universe. At least four relationships were broken through the Fall. First, Adam and Eve's intimate relationship with God was broken (Gen. 3:8–9). This was the primary relationship they had been created for, the most important aspect of their lives. When their relationship with God was broken, their other relationships were damaged too: their relationship with themselves as individuals (Gen. 3:7, 10), with each other as fellow human beings (Gen. 3:7, 12, 16), and with the rest of creation (Gen. 3:17–19). The universe is intricately designed and interwoven. It is wholistic, composed of multiple parts, each of which depends on the proper functioning of the others. All parts are governed by laws established by God. When the primary relationship between God and humanity was severed, every part of the original harmony of God's creation was affected. The results of this comprehensive brokenness have plagued humanity ever since. War, hatred, violence, environmental degradation, injustice, corruption, idolatry, poverty, and famine all spring from sin.

Thus, when God set out to restore his creation from the all-encompassing effects of man's rebellion, his redemptive plan could not be small or narrow, focusing on a single area of brokenness. His plan is not limited to saving human souls or teaching or even healing. Rather, it combines all three with the goal of restoring everything, including each of the four broken relationships described above. Colossians 1:19–20 provides a picture of God's wholistic redemptive plan: "For God was pleased to have all his fullness dwell in [Christ], and through him to reconcile to himself all things, whether things on earth or things in heaven, by making peace through his blood, shed on the cross."

God is redeeming *all things*. Through Christ's blood shed on the cross, our sins are forgiven and our fellowship with God is renewed. And not only that—we also can experience substantial healing within ourselves, with others, and with the environment. The gospel is not only good news for after we die; it is good news here and now!

Ministers of Reconciliation

The task of the church is to join God in his big agenda of restoring all things. We are "Christ's ambassadors," called to the "ministry of reconciliation" (see 2 Cor. 5:18–20). In the words of Christian apologist Francis Schaeffer, we should be working "on the basis of the finished work of Christ . . . [for] substantial healing now in every area where there are divisions because of the Fall."[6] To do this, we must first believe that such healing *can* be a reality here and now, in every area, on the basis of the finished work of Christ. This healing will not be perfect or complete on this side of Christ's return, yet it can be real, evident, and substantial.

Preaching, teaching, and substantial healing in every area where brokenness exists as a result of the Fall—in essence, wholistic ministry—is the vision that Christ had and modeled for us on earth. It was the vision that set the agenda for William Carey in India. It is the vision that should set the agenda for our ministry as well.

DISCOVERY QUESTIONS
Healing the Brokenness

To gain a deeper understanding of wholistic ministry, open your Bible and study the following passages.

1. Genesis 1:26–2:25 provides an account of God's work in creation. In this passage we learn that God created humankind to live in the context of at least three basic relationships. They can be divided into one primary relationship and two secondary relationships. In Genesis 1:26–27, what is the primary relationship? Why would this be described as the primary relationship?

_____

_____

_____

_____

2. Based on Genesis 1:26–27, what is the biblical answer to the basic human questions "Who am I?" and "What does it mean to be human?"

    _____

    _____

    _____

3. Which secondary relationship do we learn about in Genesis 2:18, 20b–25?

    _____

    _____

4. Which secondary relationship do we see in Genesis 1:26, 28–30?

    _____

    _____

5. Read Genesis 3:8–10. What do these verses indicate about Adam and Eve's primary relationship with God? What effects of this have you seen in the world around you?

    _____

    _____

    _____

6. Read Genesis 3:11–13, 16–19. What happened to Adam and Eve's secondary relationships after their primary relationship with God was broken? What effects of this have you seen in the world today? See also Romans 8:19–21.

    _____

    _____

_____

_____

_____

7. Read Colossians 1:19–20. What is God's response to the world's comprehensive brokenness? According to this passage, why did Jesus die on the cross?

_____

_____

_____

8. According to 2 Corinthians 5:18–20, what is our role as Christians in God's redemptive plan?

_____

_____

_____

9. Read 2 Timothy 4:2 and 1 John 3:11, 16–18. What specific things can we do to fulfill our part in God's plan?

_____

_____

_____

_____

10. Examine Isaiah 25:6–8 and Revelation 21:1–5. Will God's redemptive plan be accomplished? List the kinds of healing that will occur in the relationships broken through the Fall (God-to-human, human-to-human, and human-to-creation).

_____

_____

_____

_____

KEY POINTS TO REMEMBER
Wholistic Ministry in Review

1. The "whole" of Christian ministry is the advancement of God's kingdom and the discipling of the nations. The parts include preaching, teaching, and healing.
2. Without these three parts working together from the basis of a biblical worldview, our ministry is less than what Christ intends and will lack power to transform lives and communities.
3. To understand wholistic ministry, we must recognize the comprehensive impact of the Fall and God's big agenda in history to redeem all things broken through the Fall.
4. Four fundamental relationships were broken through the Fall: (1) the relationship between God and humans, (2) human individuals' relationship with themselves, (3) the relationship between fellow humans, and (4) the relationship between humans and the environment.
5. God's redemptive plan is comprehensive and includes the restoration and healing of everything broken through the Fall, including the four fundamental relationships.

CLOSING THOUGHTS
Functionally Separate, Relationally Inseparable

When Jesus sent out his disciples on their first missionary journey, "he sent them out to preach the kingdom of God and to heal the sick" (Luke 9:2). Yet today it's common for Christian ministries to separate the twin ministry components. Some focus exclusively on preaching, evangelism, or church planting, while others focus on meeting the physical needs of the broken or impoverished. Typically these two groups have little interaction. This division is not what Christ intended. By focusing on one to the exclusion of the other, ministries are limited and ineffective in bringing about true, lasting transformation.

The Bible provides a model of ministry where preaching, teaching, and healing are, in the words of Dr. Tetsunao Yamamori, "functionally separate, yet relationally inseparable."[7] Each part is distinct and deserves special attention and focus. Yet the parts *must* function together. Together they form a wholistic ministry that is both powerful and effective—a ministry able to transform lives and entire nations. The work of William Carey in India gives historical testimony to this fact. According to theologian David Wells, preaching, teaching, and healing must be "inextricably related to each other, the former being the foundation and the latter being the evidence of the working of the former."[8]

PERSONAL APPLICATION
The Body of Christ

The apostle Paul taught that the church is the body of Christ and each part of the body depends on the other parts for the whole to function as God intends (Rom. 12:4–8). These parts are spiritual gifts, skills, and interests, many of which correspond to the three essential elements of wholistic ministry we examined in this session: preaching (evangelism), teaching (discipleship), and healing (compassionate, practical ministry to the poor and broken). Use the following questions to examine wholistic ministry.

1. Read Romans 12:6–8. What gifts in this passage relate to preaching, teaching, and healing?

     _____

     _____

     _____

     _____

2. Give an example of Christians with different gifts working together in wholistic ministry. What impact did this have?

     _____

     _____

     _____

3. Give an example of a ministry effort that was not wholistic. What parts were lacking? What was the result?

_____

_____

_____

_____

4. Do you think the concept of wholistic ministry is widely understood by your fellow Christians? If so, is it widely practiced? If not, why not?

_____

_____

_____

_____

5. Of the three basic areas of wholistic ministry (preaching, teaching, and practical ministry), which do you believe God has best equipped you to do?

_____

_____

_____

_____

6. What are you currently doing to exercise your gifts? Are you doing it in a way that reflects wholistic ministry? What practical steps could help make your ministry efforts more wholistic?

_____

_____

_____

_____

The next session: *obstacles to wholistic ministry*

Obstacles to Wholistic Ministry

Born in Northern Ireland to a wealthy Presbyterian family, Amy Carmichael (1867–1951) became one of the best-known missionaries of the first half of the twentieth century. Her ministry took her first to Japan, then to Sri Lanka (Ceylon at the time), and finally to Dohnavur in South India. By the time Carmichael arrived in India, the murder of widows through immolation had been legally banned as a result of the tenacious efforts of the pioneer British missionary William Carey. Yet Carmichael was horrified to discover that ritual abortion and female infanticide were still commonly practiced. Also, many of the young women were being sold to the nearby pagan temples to be cult prostitutes.

Within a few years of her arrival in India, Carmichael established a ministry to protect and shelter these girls. Although she had to suffer the persecution of various Hindu sects and the bureaucratic resistance of the British colonial government, she built an effective and dynamic ministry renowned for its courage and compassion. Sadly, many of her fellow missionaries in India believed that her efforts to build an orphanage and school were "worldly activities" that distracted her from the "saving of souls." To such accusations she simply replied, "Souls are more or less firmly attached to bodies."[1]

The negative reaction of Carmichael's fellow missionaries toward her efforts to care for Indian women highlights a dispute that has torn the church for over a century. Carmichael was part of the historic missionary movement that deployed hundreds of European and American missionaries to nearly every continent on earth. These missionaries succeeded in establishing millions of new churches. However, many of these missionaries believed that evangelism should be the sole purpose of ministry. Efforts to offer assistance to the poor or to bring about social reform in line with biblical truth were viewed with suspicion and seen as activities that Christians should either avoid or make a low priority.

Many of these nineteenth and twentieth century missionaries were reacting against a growing movement. Sometimes referred to as the "social gospel," this movement abandoned the biblical teaching of human sinfulness and the need for spiritual redemption. Many of its adherents believed the kingdom of God could be established on earth through human efforts— primarily in the form of government-sponsored programs and progressive social reforms. For those within this movement, evangelism (negatively referred to as "proselytizing") was intrusive, insensitive, and ultimately unnecessary. In the words of American newspaperman and social gospel proponent Horace Greeley, "The heart of man is not depraved . . . his passions do not prompt to wrong doing, and do not therefore by their actions, produce evil."[2]

Amy Carmichael sought to practice a biblically balanced wholistic ministry and, in so doing, found herself in the midst of a great debate. On one side were those, like her fellow missionaries, who believed that evangelism alone should define the mission of the church. Others, like Horace Greeley, no longer believed in the need for evangelism, arguing that humans were masters of their own destiny and that social reorganization held the key to establishing God's kingdom. The loser in this debate was the biblical vision of wholistic ministry that Amy Carmichael understood and practiced, and the ministry of the church was gravely weakened as a result.

Fragmented, dichotomized, and ultimately unbiblical ministry efforts are still commonplace today. These efforts, in many cases, are unable to effect lasting transformation in people and nations. (For more background on the historical basis for this conflict, please refer to "A Brief History of the Divided Mind and Life" in the appendix.)

KEY WORDS TO KNOW
False Foundations

Gnosticism

Rooted in Greek philosophy and developed by various sects around the time of Christ, Gnosticism is a belief system that dichotomizes matter and spirit, treating the material realm as illusory and evil. For Gnostics, salvation came by acquiring spiritual knowledge (the root word *gnosis* means "knowledge"), which liberates the spirit from the body. Gnosticism directly opposed the biblical worldview, which holds that the material world—including the human body—was created good. The early Gnostics were scandalized by the doctrine of the incarnation, God in human flesh. Because they modified or rejected basic tenets of biblical faith, they were declared heretics by the early church, and yet certain Gnostic assumptions about the material world continue to plague the church today.

Proselytize

Today, the word *proselytize* generally means the act of inducing someone to convert to one's own faith through direct or indirect coercion or pressure.

Materialism

Materialism is a belief system which holds that all reality can be reduced to the physical or material and thus excludes a spiritual or supernatural realm. There is no God or gods and no spirit or soul. This belief system is also called naturalism or secularism.

KEY VERSES TO READ
One, the Other, or Both?

I give you this charge: Preach the Word; be prepared in season and out of season; correct, rebuke and encourage—with great patience and careful instruction.

—2 Timothy 4:1–2

Dear children, let us not love with words or tongue but with actions and in truth.

—1 John 3:18

1. What are the two components of ministry outlined in these verses?

   _____

   _____

2. What did the apostle John warn against?

   _____

   _____

3. What happens to our ministry when one or the other component is neglected?

   _____

   _____

   _____

BIBLICAL INSIGHTS
Three Obstacles

The same resistance that Amy Carmichael faced from her fellow missionaries remains with us today. A conflict has torn at the church in our generation regarding the very nature of its ministry in the world. When Christian ministry efforts are compartmentalized, the whole to which they all contribute—glorifying God and advancing his kingdom—is lost. There are three obstacles to balanced, wholistic Christian ministry.

Overemphasizing Evangelism

Many Christians today give priority to evangelism, preaching the gospel, reaching the unreached, and starting new churches. These activities are essential to biblical ministry, yet they are only part of a greater whole. By focusing exclusively on evangelism and church planting, some Christians begin to view new converts and new churches as ends in themselves. In reality, these things are means to a greater end—the transformation of nations and the advancement of God's kingdom. When we hear testimonies of new converts and new churches planted, our response should be one of praise to God and affirmation of the work. But we should also ask, Do they have God's vision for their lives, their families, and their nations? Do they understand their strategic role in social transformation? Or will they neglect ministry to the poor and broken and isolate themselves from the public square?

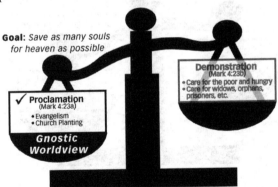

Evangelism was never meant to be separated from discipleship, care for the needy, and social transformation. Well-known British Bible scholar John Stott has observed that the church in many parts of the world today is "characterized by superficiality. The Christian situation is strange, tragic and possessing a disturbing paradox. In some places, the church is growing strongly, but even there, the problem is that the growth is without depth."[3] Why is this so? Could it be that we have unintentionally abandoned a biblical worldview in favor of Gnostic assumptions that are antithetical to wholism and wholistic ministry? If so, we must return to a robust biblical worldview and discard such assumptions. We must make it our all-consuming passion to see God's glory reflected in every sphere of our society. Then we will see evangelism and church planting in their proper contexts, as means to this larger end.

Overemphasizing Social Ministry

While some Christians today focus on evangelism at the expense of discipleship and care for the needy, others do the opposite, emphasizing social ministry at the expense of evangelism. For such Christians, evangelism is seen as "proselytizing" and is to be avoided. People, they believe, are not "lost" or in need of salvation but are inherently good. Evil is not rooted in fallen human hearts but in unjust, inequitable social structures.

This group has also lost the whole vision of biblical ministry. Glorifying God and advancing his kingdom are replaced with social justice and universal prosperity. God never intended ministry to the poor to be separated from evangelism and discipleship. When such separation occurs, the biblical foundation of wholistic ministry is replaced by the worldview of materialism. According to this belief system, God (if he exists at all) is a distant, passive deity who is uninvolved in the affairs of this world. The Bible is not revered as God's "living and active" word (Heb. 4:12), the source of authoritative instruction in all areas of life. Instead, it is little more than a devotional text, intended to inspire and motivate. God has left the job of establishing his kingdom in our capable hands. If enough money, technology, or enlightened government policies are focused on the right problems, then poverty and injustice will surely be eliminated.

Today, such thinking is commonplace in many "community development" organizations, including those founded by Christians. These organizations tend to be staffed with highly trained professionals who apply the latest knowledge and techniques in the areas of food production, water resource development, and preventative medicine.

Although these efforts have resulted in many short-term benefits, they have failed to effect long-term transformation. Recent studies—as shown in books like *Dead Aid: How Aid Is Not Working and How There Is a Better Way for Africa* by Dambisa Moyo, and *The White Man's Burden: Why the West's Efforts to Aid the Rest Have Done So Much Ill and So Little Good* by William Easterly—reveal that despite the best of intentions, aid efforts have in many cases resulted in greater dependency from and long-term damage to the people they intend to help. These well-intentioned efforts fail because they are built on a false foundation. They neglect the clear biblical teaching that the human race is broken and separated from God. Our best knowledge, resources, and technology will never be enough to heal all of the world's brokenness. Our only hope rests with the supernatural and complete healing available through the cross of Christ.

Misguided Wholism

Many Christians today recognize the errors of both those who overemphasize evangelism and those who overemphasize social ministry. Yet in their attempt to address the errors, they sometimes unintentionally stumble into another problem—misguided wholism. A misguided wholistic ministry attempts to "add" evangelistic activities (rooted in Gnostic assumptions) to community development activities (rooted in materialistic assumptions).

Goal: Save as many souls for heaven as possible

Goal: Help as many poor and hungry people as possible

CONFLICT!

Proclamation (Mark 4:23a)

+

Relief and Development (Mark 4:23b)

✓ Evangelism
✓ Church planting

✓ Care for the poor, hungry, the widows etc.

Gnostic Worldview ✛ Secular Worldview

How do we see this "adding" taking place? In some ministry organizations, separate departments are created, one focusing on evangelism and the other on social ministry. In other cases, mission organizations partner with community development organizations, attempting to combine their areas of expertise in a particular community or region. Such attempts at adding evangelism to community development or vise versa rarely work because the two groups will often have conflicting assumptions and differing visions and ultimate objectives. While attempting to work in a coordinated way, each group may quietly believe that its expertise is vital while the other's is not. The inevitable result is mistrust and conflict. The two parts lack a unified vision of the whole and each is rooted in incompatible assumptions about reality. Trying to mix Gnostic evangelism with materialistic community development is like trying to mix oil and water. While such efforts may appear wholistic on the surface, they will fail because of irreconcilable divisions that are never dealt with.

We have examined three obstacles to biblical, wholistic ministry, three pitfalls to avoid. Unfortunately, these pitfalls are so common that it is difficult to find contemporary examples of genuine wholistic ministry. Such models do exist, but most remain in the annals of church history. We need to move forward by looking back, rediscovering the beauty and power of wholistic ministry from the pages of our own history. We have already looked at the examples of heroic men and women of faith like Amy

Carmichael, William Carey, and Abraham Kuyper, and we have briefly examined Christ's ministry and the ministry of the apostles. These short studies can be a starting point for continued independent learning about wholistic ministry.

DISCOVERY QUESTIONS
Being "Re-Minded"

Perhaps you've identified with one of the three pitfalls described in this lesson. Perhaps your personal ministry, your church's ministry, or the ministry organization you serve with lacks a wholistic approach. Use the following questions to discover what the Bible says about change and repentance.

1. Read Romans 12:2. What is the threefold pattern found in this verse?

    _____

    _____

    _____

2. The word *transformed* is equivalent to the Greek word *metamorphoun*, from which the English word *metamorphosis* is derived. What is an example of something in the natural world that experiences a metamorphosis? What does it mean to be transformed?

    _____

    _____

    _____

3. According to Romans 12:2, if my life (my behavior) and my ministry efforts are to be transformed, what must take place first?

    _____

    _____

    _____

4. Read John 8:31–32. What must a person do to be a disciple of Jesus?

_____

_____

5. Notice the "if-then" relationship between John 8:31 and 8:32. This is a conditional promise. God gives a promise, but it will occur only as the condition is fulfilled. What is the progressive twofold promise?

    If _____

    _____

    Then _____

    _____

6. Why is being a devoted student of God's Word essential to practicing wholistic ministry?

    _____

    _____

    _____

7. Read Leviticus 4:13. Is it possible to sin unintentionally?

    _____

8. Read 1 John 1:8–2:2. If you become aware of an unintentional sin in your life, what should you do? What will God do as a result?

    _____

    _____

    _____

KEY POINTS TO REMEMBER
The Obstacles to Wholistic Ministry in Review

1. Wholistic ministry is founded on a balanced, biblical worldview in which evangelistic ministry and social ministry are valued together.
2. Some Christians, influenced by Gnosticism, overemphasize evangelism,

preaching the gospel, and starting new churches and wrongly minimize or neglect ministry to broken, poor, and needy people.

3. Other Christians, influenced by materialism, overemphasize social ministry and view evangelism as proselytizing. This group wrongly assumes that people are basically good and that evil is rooted not in fallen human hearts but in unjust, inequitable social structures.

4. Misguided wholistic ministry tries to combine Gnostic evangelism with materialistic social ministry and usually fails because the parts lack the common foundation of a biblical worldview and the common goal of glorifying God and advancing his kingdom.

CLOSING THOUGHTS
The Need to Repent

There is a solution. If we discover that we are stuck in one of the pitfalls discussed in this session, we can repent. To repent means to be "reminded," to change both our mind and our ways. With God's help we can deliberately cast off the unbiblical, compartmentalized mindset that has held us in its grip and return to a way of thinking that is informed by the biblical worldview—a mindset of wholism. Does this sound overwhelming? It would be without God's grace and power and the guidance of the Holy Spirit. As we repent and seek to walk in his ways, he will direct our paths and make our lives and ministries what he wants them to be—biblical, effective, and powerful—to bring him glory and to advance his kingdom.

PERSONAL APPLICATION
Consider Your Ministry Experience

Use the questions below to consider your own ministry experience. Has it reflected biblical wholism?

1. Have you been involved in a ministry that emphasized evangelism, emphasized social ministry, or attempted to combine the two? If so, what were the positive results of this effort?

_____

_____

_____

_____

What were the negative results of this effort?

_____

_____

_____

_____

What do you think could have been done differently (or should be done differently in the future)?

_____

_____

_____

_____

2. Consider your current or future ministry opportunities. In what practical ways can you repent, changing your objectives or practices to reflect a wholistic mindset?

_____

_____

_____

_____

3. Schedule a time to earnestly seek God's guidance, alone or together with your ministry team. Ask God, "What do you want my/our ministry to look like? How can I/we best serve your kingdom purposes?" Listen and wait for God to speak; then write down what you learn.

_____

_____

_____

_____

_____

_____

_____

_____

_____

_____

_____

_____

The next session: *the essentials of wholistic ministry*

Wholistic Ministry Essentials

The Pokomchi Indians are among the poorest people in the poorest state of Guatemala. Many years ago missionaries came to evangelize and start churches in Pokomchi communities. At that time many accepted Christ as their Savior, yet they remained desperately poor. The young Christian converts gained hope for the future, but no hope for today. In fact, they were literally waiting to die so they could leave their miserable existence on earth and go to be with Jesus in heaven. Several years later community development organizations came to work with the Pokomchi, interested in helping them improve their living conditions. They brought in resources from materially wealthy countries and completed many projects, labeling them successful. Now there were latrines, but they were largely unused. There were school buildings, but very few children attended or graduated. Many of the projects that were to improve the physical condition of the Pokomchi were completed, but there was no transformation in the lives and communities of the Pokomchi. The people remained dreadfully poor.

In the early 1990s a young Peruvian pastor named Arturo began his ministry to the Pokomchi. Unlike the earlier missionaries and community development professionals, Arturo understood the importance of the biblical worldview for individual and community transformation. He understood that authentic Christian ministry is to be wholistic—seeking to bring healing and restoration to every area of brokenness in the community. He began to work with illiterate Pokomchi pastors. He took them through a comprehensive study of the Bible in hopes of challenging their fatalistic mindsets. Arturo believed that true repentance involves more than trusting Christ as Savior to gain access to heaven. It also requires a transformed mindset, leading to a transformed life.

As Arturo taught the pastors from the Bible, he used everyday illustrations to teach concepts like God's intention for mankind to exercise dominion and stewardship over creation. One of the primary causes of malnutrition in the Pokomchi communities was the lack of proper storage facilities for harvested crops. Often local farmers harvested a good crop, only to have rats eat it before their children could be fed. Arturo asked the farmers, "Who is smarter, you or the rats?" The farmers nervously laughed as they concluded, "The rats." Arturo asked, "Do you have dominion over the rats, or do the rats have dominion over your lives?" The farmers reluctantly acknowledged that, at least as far as crop storage was concerned, the rats had dominion over them. Then Arturo pointed out the biblical truth that men and women are image-bearers of God and have been given dominion over creation. Just as God is creative (he created the heavens and the earth), humans also possess creativity. With their God-given creativity and a proper understanding of their role to subdue and care for creation, they could overcome their food storage problem.

Gradually the fatalistic mindset of the Pokomchi pastors was transformed into one of trust and hope. Their churches were impacted as a result. Through these churches, their communities began to change dramatically. Children started to attend school because the people began to value education, particularly education in God's Word. Women learned to read because they understood that God cares equally for men and women. Men began to try new farming techniques because they wanted to be good stewards of what God provided. Women built stoves in their homes so their children would not fall into open cooking fires and get burned. Women also began to create small pantries to keep insects and vermin out of their food supplies because they understood their responsibility to exercise stewardship and provide for their communities.

When a seminary professor from the United States visited Arturo on one occasion, he was stunned and overjoyed to see the transformation that had occurred—transformation that was the result of wholistic ministry, based on the power of biblical truth applied to all areas of life. Tears welled up in his eyes and he said, "Surely the kingdom of God has come to the Pokomchi!"

KEY VERSES TO READ

Wholistic Growth

> Jesus grew in wisdom and stature, and in favor with God and men.
>
> —*Luke 2:52*

1. In what four ways did Jesus grow?

   _____

   _____

2. From the perspective of the Bible, how does a person grow in wisdom? in stature? in favor with God? in favor with men?

   _____

   _____

   _____

   _____

3. What is significant about Luke's highlighting these four areas of Jesus' growth? What does it mean for your growth? for the growth of others?

   _____

   _____

   _____

4. Did Jesus' growth happen immediately, or was it a process?

_____

_____

BIBLICAL INSIGHTS
Six Essentials

Wholistic ministry is not a technique or a fad. It is the natural out-growth of a wholistic life, one that understands that God is a real, active, all-powerful, loving presence, and lives in total devotion to him. A life that recognizes Jesus as King of kings and Lord of lords, not just in a future heavenly realm, but now. A life that appreciates that he is not merely Lord of the spiritual realm but Lord over *everything* in creation.

Let's examine six essentials of truly wholistic ministry: (1) the whole vision, (2) the whole Word, (3) the whole person, (4) the whole world, (5) motivated by love, and (6) dependent on God's strength.

I. The Whole Vision

"Vision" is the ability to "see" a preferred future state with the eyes of the mind. It is a basic human need, for it motivates and provides hope for the future. It provides a target at which we can aim our lives. Scripture affirms that "where there is no vision, the people perish" (Prov. 29:18 KJV).

Jesus was driven by a vision, not just any vision, but the grandest vision the world has ever known. His eyes saw beyond the present reality of death and injustice, to a world purified of all evil and full of the reality of God (Rev. 21:1–5). A world transformed by his loving Father who is actively at work in history, redeeming all things—one person, one family, one church, and one nation at a time. This was the vision for which he "lived, labored, suffered and died. It's this vision he entrusted to his disciples."[1] It must be our vision as well, but is it? The great missionary-statesman E. Stanley Jones offered this sad assessment: "The Church has lost it. The Church has lost [the biblical vision of] the Kingdom of God."[2] He called this loss "the sickness of our age."

Today, the *whole* kingdom vision of Jesus has been replaced by incomplete visions. For some, Christ's grand vision has been reduced to saving souls from every nation, which provides little hope for people living in desperate brokenness and poverty—only hope after they die. To be sure, the biblical vision of God's kingdom provides eternal hope, but it also holds hope for substantial healing now.

For others, Christ's vision is reduced to ending hunger, poverty, and injustice. If this is the entire vision, it is far too limited. People need more than full stomachs and safe environments. They need a vision that addresses their spiritual hunger as well as their physical hunger, a vision that holds hope not only for a better life on earth but for eternal life as well. People need a vision that calls them to something higher than simply having their basic physical needs met. People everywhere are searching for a vision that they can live and die for, a purpose worthy of their entire devotion. Jesus addressed this when he said, "Man does not live on bread alone, but on every word that comes from the mouth of God" (Matt. 4:4). To practice wholistic ministry, it is essential that we have the *whole* vision that Jesus had, not the incomplete visions so common today. His ultimate aim is expressed in these words from the Lord's Prayer, "Your kingdom come, your will be done on earth as it is in heaven" (Matt. 6:10).

2. The Whole Word

Where does this whole vision come from? It comes from a comprehensive understanding of God's Word. God's revealed truth in Scripture is inspired and divinely powerful. It is his "transforming story," equally valid for all cultures, all nations, and all time. As we read the whole Bible from Genesis to Revelation, not as a series of disconnected stories and teachings but as a single, comprehensive narrative, our minds are transformed (Rom. 12:2). We come to understand the truth about God, creation, history, and our lives.

The Bible reveals that God is actively working in history, carrying out a magnificent plan to bless, heal, and redeem everything broken through the Fall. This plan is the central theme of the *entire* Bible. It's the common thread that unites both Old and New Testaments, beginning immediately after Adam and Eve's separation from God in Genesis 3 and concluding in the final chapters of Revelation. Why did God make his covenant with Abraham? Why did he create and bless the nation of Israel? Why did he send his Son Jesus to live among us and die on the cross? Why did he raise up the church? What does he want to accomplish through this church in our generation? What vision should guide and give purpose and meaning to our lives? For the answer to each of these questions, we need to understand God's big agenda—his history-encompassing redemptive plan for the nations.

To appreciate the scope of this remarkable plan, it is important to study more than passages or even a book in the Bible. We must look at and study the Scriptures as a complete, unified whole. We need to capture a bird's-eye view of the Bible and understand its "big picture." According to British theologian John Stott, we must have "a mind which has firmly grasped the basic presuppositions of Scripture and is thoroughly informed with biblical truth."[3]

3. The Whole Person

To practice wholistic ministry, it is essential that we see people as Jesus sees them, not as disembodied "souls," not as evolving physical machines with no spirit, but as a wholistic integration of body, mind, and spirit. To reduce people to any one of these parts, or even to say that one is more important than the others, cannot be supported in Scripture. God cares for whole people, and so must we.

In the key verse for this session we looked at the growth of Jesus in four distinct areas. He grew *physically*—"in stature." His physical body grew strong and healthy. He grew *mentally*—"in wisdom." He grew in the knowledge of God and his Word. He grew *spiritually*—"in favor with God." He had an intimate relationship with his Father. He grew *socially*—"in favor with men." He attracted a loyal band of followers and was esteemed by many for his wisdom, power, humility, and compassion. All these areas were equally important in Jesus' development. Therefore they must be equally important for us and for all people. Wholistic ministry sees in Jesus the perfect model for human development. If our ministry fails to help people grow in any of these areas, it's not wholistic.

Luke 2:52 also reveals that Jesus lived in the context of relationships. As he matured, he grew "in favor with God and men." In the same way, our lives are lived in the context of relationships. Scripture identifies one of these relationships as the most important—our relationship to God. We are his creation, made in his image, and fashioned to enjoy an intimate, eternal relationship with him. The central problem we face (and the central problem for the whole world) is that our relationship with God is broken and in need of reconciliation. The good news is that "God so loved the world that he gave his one and only Son, that whoever believes in him shall not perish but have eternal life" (John 3:16). Thanks to God's initiative, we can now enjoy renewed fellowship with him through faith in his Son and his atoning death on the cross.

Spiritual rebirth is essential for wholistic ministry (John 3:3). Only when our relationship with God is restored will there be lasting hope for healing in our other relationships—both our relationship with creation and with other people. Wholistic ministry is concerned with *all* these relationships, yet it never forgets what the primary relationship is. It cares for the whole needs of whole people in the context of all their relationships, but this care always begins with a deep concern for people's need to be reconciled to their Maker.

4. The Whole World

In his Great Commission, Jesus commanded, "Go and make disciples of all nations" (Matt. 28:19). Later he told his disciples that they would "be [his] witnesses in Jerusalem, and in all Judea and Samaria, and to the ends of the earth" (Acts 1:8). The gospel of Jesus Christ is to be proclaimed in every nation on earth. It is also to bring healing and transformation to the nations it impacts. A ministry that is wholistic seeks both parts. It works to spread the gospel to every nation *and* to have "God's glory reflected in every domain of the land, its arts, sciences, media,

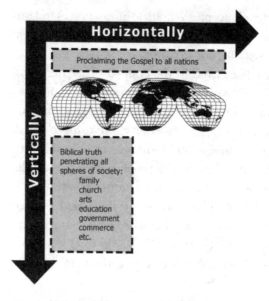

government, schools, businesses, [and] families."[4]

Psalm 24:1 says, "The earth is the LORD's, and everything in it, the world, and all who live in it." Abraham Kuyper famously paraphrased this verse when he said, "There is not a square inch of the universe over which King Jesus does not claim, 'Mine!'" A ministry that is wholistic is driven by this motto. It sets its agenda with questions like, If Jesus were mayor of my community, what would be different? If Jesus were ruler of my nation, what changes would he make? If God's will were perfectly done "on earth as it is in heaven," what would change? Once we have answers to these questions, we know what our ministry must address.

5. Motivated by Love

As we seek to practice wholistic ministry, we must keep in mind Jesus' great commandment: "Love the Lord your God with all your heart and with all your soul and with all your mind . . . [and] love your neighbor as yourself" (Matt. 22:37–39). Our ministry must be motivated by love for God and for others, particularly for those who are poverty-stricken, broken, and hopeless. The essence of the Christian life is found in seeking to glorify God and seeking the best for others. It is striving always to improve the lives of people spiritually, physically, emotionally, economically, and socially. In the words of Dr. James M. Boice, "We are called to sincere, selfless, sacrificial, serving love."[5] One of the truly revolutionary aspects of Christian faith is that we show our love for God primarily through our love for our neighbor (Isa. 58:6–12; Matt. 7:12; 25:31–46). No matter how many good works we do, without love we will accomplish nothing. In the timeless words of the apostle Paul, "If I give all I possess to the poor and surrender my body to the flames, but have not love, I gain nothing" (1 Cor. 13:3).

6. Dependent on God's Strength

The final essential factor is dependence on God. To be effective in wholistic ministry, we must remember that God is actively advancing his kingdom right now. Our attitude must be one of joining him, not setting off on our own. We must act in his strength, not our own, for if we strive in our own strength, wit, or wisdom, we will surely fail. We may believe we have succeeded at some level and be tempted to take credit for ourselves. Such pride has no place in biblical Christianity. We are dependent on God for every breath we take. We must remember that for our ministry to bear fruit, our lives must be firmly connected to Christ's life. Jesus spoke of this in the parable of the vine and the branches. "I am the vine; you are the branches. If a man remains in me and I in him, he will bear much fruit; apart from me you can do nothing" (John 15:5). How do we stay connected to the vine? By realizing that he is our active leader, practicing moment by moment dependence on him, and expressing our dependence through prayer, sensitivity to the leading of the Holy Spirit, and obedience to his Word. We are meant to carry out wholistic ministry together with God as he acts with us, not on our own. "He [desires] to be our constant companion or coworker in the creative enterprise of life on earth," theologian Dallas Willard reminds us. "What we can do by our unassisted strength is very small. What we can do acting with mechanical, electrical or atomic power is much greater. . . . But what we can do with these means is still very small compared to what we could do acting in union with God himself, who created and ultimately controls all other forces."[6]

DISCOVERY QUESTIONS
A Deeper Understanding of Ministry Essentials

Open your Bible and learn more about the essentials of wholistic ministry.

1. Begin by reading Luke 4:43. For what purpose was Jesus sent? What does this tell you about the importance of the kingdom to Jesus?

   _____

   _____

   _____

   Do you share the same purpose? Does your church?

   _____

   _____

   _____

2. Read John 12:27–28. Within hours of going to the cross, how did Jesus express his ultimate purpose? What does this reveal about what our ultimate purpose ought to be?

   _____

   _____

   _____

3. Read Isaiah 11:6–9 and 25:6–8. What do these passages say about God's intentions for the future? How do they help you understand the vision that drove the ministry of Jesus?

   _____

   _____

   _____

   _____

4. Read Matthew 25:31–40. What is the relationship between the love of God and our response to people's needs? Do you think it is possible to share the love of God without helping meet people's needs? Explain your answer.

   _____

   _____

   _____

5. Read Psalm 82:3–4, Isaiah 58:6–7, and James 1:27. What do these passages say are biblical responses to human needs or problems? Are they things that you and your church are capable of doing?

    _____

    _____

    _____

    _____

6. Read Matthew 4:4 and John 6:51. What other kind of food do people need in order to live? Why do people need both physical and spiritual food? Is one more important than the other? What happens when one or the other is neglected?

    _____

    _____

    _____

    _____

7. Read Jeremiah 17:5 and John 15:5. What do these passages tell us about how we are to carry out ministry?

    _____

    _____

    _____

8. Read 1 Peter 4:11. What is the ultimate purpose of our service or ministry? How do we serve so that God is glorified?

    _____

    _____

    _____

KEY POINTS TO REMEMBER
A Review of the Essentials

1. We must have a whole vision. Jesus was driven by a vision that aimed first and foremost at glorifying God. His ultimate aim is expressed in

the Lord's Prayer: "Your Kingdom come, your will be done on earth as it is in heaven" (Matt. 6:10).

2. We must embrace the whole Word. The big picture of the Bible is God's redemptive plan in history. We must see it as a comprehensive worldview that holds the power to transform entire nations.

3. We must see and minister to the whole person. People are a unity of body, mind, and spirit living in the context of a set of relationships, the most important of which is their relationship to God.

4. We must see the whole world, preaching God's Word to people from every nation. The gospel brings healing and transformation to every domain of culture.

5. We must be motivated by love. At the core of wholistic ministry is a burning desire to glorify God and seek the best for others.

6. We must be dependent on God's strength. Wholistic ministry is first and foremost God's business. We must realize our moment by moment dependence on him and express this dependence through prayer, sensitivity to his leading, and obedience to his Word.

CLOSING THOUGHTS

A Concise Description of Wholistic Ministry

Pastor and author John Piper offers this helpful definition of spiritual leadership, which also serves as a one-sentence description of wholistic ministry: "Leadership is knowing where God wants people to be and taking the initiative to get them there by *God's* means in reliance on *God's* power."[7] Where does God want people to be? Piper says, "We find out where God wants people to be [by asking] where God himself is going."[8] We must understand God's vision—his big agenda in history—especially for mankind. He desires that his kingdom come and his will be done on earth as it is in heaven (Matt. 6:10). This was the reason that Christ came to the earth and died on the cross (Luke 4:43). He desires all men to come to a saving knowledge of him and be healed spiritually, physically, socially, and mentally. He desires all of this for the sake of his glory (John 12:28). This must be our vision and our motivation as well.

How do we achieve this vision? Do we rely on money or human wisdom? Do we rely on accepted professional practices? No. We must rely on God's means, which are likely very different from ours. We discover his means through his Word as we seek to apply it to every area of life and culture.

Yet having the right vision, motivation, and means is still not enough. We must also work "in reliance on his power." In the end, we must realize that we have nothing in our flesh—in our human wisdom or power—that is of any value in advancing God's grand redemptive agenda (Isa. 2:22; Ps. 146:3). We must realize that everything we have comes from him, and then work in his power (John 15:5). We must work to advance his glory and not our own. These are the essentials of wholistic ministry.

PERSONAL APPLICATION

Applying the Essentials

God wants each of us to glorify him by participating in his big agenda of advancing the kingdom. We do this as we understand and apply biblical truth in our whole lives and as we love our neighbors and God's creation through wholistic ministry. Use these questions to apply this lesson's principles to your ministry efforts.

1. Which of the essentials discussed in this session do you believe your church understands and practices as it ministers in your community? (Review the "Key Points" section for a quick overview of these essentials.)

    _____

    _____

    _____

2. Which essentials do you think your church lacks or is weak in?

    _____

    _____

    _____

3. Which of the essentials discussed in this session do you believe you understand and practice as you minister to others?

    _____

    _____

    _____

    _____

4. Which essentials do you lack or are you weak in?

    _____

    _____

    _____

    _____

5. Based on what you've learned in this session, what are some things you could do to help your church understand and practice wholistic ministry? What things could you do to improve your own ministry efforts?

    _____

    _____

    _____

    _____

    _____

    _____

A Brief History of the Divided Mind and Life

An Ancient Heresy

The sacred-secular dichotomy that shapes the mindset of many Christians today is nearly as old as the church itself. Its roots can be traced back to ancient Greek philosophy, and to the ideas of Plato in particular. Plato divided creation into two self-existing and eternal parts: the spiritual was considered superior, while the material was inferior.

Plato's worldview stands in direct opposition to the Hebrew worldview, which holds that nothing except God exists from all eternity. Physical matter is not eternal. It is created by God, who is spirit. And God, who is altogether good, righteous, and perfect, declares his creation to be good as well (Gen. 1:31). The Bible affirms a distinction between physical and spiritual aspects of reality. It does not, however, declare that one realm is good while the other is evil. The biblical

worldview affirms that God is the Lord of all of creation, both physical and spiritual.

In the early church the blending of the Hebraic and Platonic (Greek) worldviews became known as the Gnostic heresy. Christians who fell within its grip struggled with the doctrine of the incarnation. How could a perfect, righteous God take on a disorderly, corrupt, physical body? Their belief system forced them to abandon this most central of all Christian doctrines; thus Gnosticism is rightly viewed as a heresy.

Yet, sadly, this same Gnostic view has continued to plague the church down through the centuries—and has experienced a marked revival over the past one hundred years. The fact that we must talk about "wholistic" ministry today is a testimony to the fact that the Gnostic mindset is alive and well. What led to the reemergence of this ancient heresy, and what have been the consequences?

The Age of Reason

The roots of modern Gnosticism can be traced to eighteenth-century Europe and a period commonly referred to as the Age of Reason or the Enlightenment. The modern scientific method was perfected during this period, with remarkable results. Great mysteries of the inner workings of the physical universe were being solved one by one with breathtaking speed. Modern science was born out of a biblical framework that affirmed creation as God's handiwork and thus worthy of exploration and study. Early scientists such as Francis Bacon, Johannes Kepler, and Sir Isaac Newton were devout Christians. They viewed their work as affirming and strengthening their biblical beliefs.

During the Enlightenment, however, an enchantment with the successes of science led to the belief that through unaided human reason man could understand the workings of the entire physical universe. Like Adam and Eve's first sin in the Garden of Eden, a prideful human confidence emerged. Man, through science and reason alone, could become like God and understand all reality.

The biblical worldview had been deeply influential in shaping European culture throughout the Middle Ages. But with the advent of the Enlightenment, it began to erode and was eventually dislodged from its prominent position. God was still the Creator and necessary "First Cause" of the universe, yet he was seen as uninvolved and irrelevant. The new worldview that was birthed during this period, known as deism, acknowledged a god who created but no longer played a role in the day-to-day functioning of the physical world. The god of deism is not lord or redeemer, because deism allows no role for the miraculous or for spiritual intervention. Prayer is unnecessary because god either cannot or will not intervene in human affairs. Many leading Enlightenment figures, including Voltaire, David Hume, and Thomas Jefferson, saw the universe as a huge, intricate machine, like a giant clock, with god serving as nothing more than the clockmaker. He made it, wound it up, and left it to run on its own.

The French Revolution (1789–1799) is emblematic of this shift in worldview. The revolutionaries sought more than political freedom; they sought to be free from God and from the narrowness and authority of the official state church.

As the Enlightenment wore on, the European mind claimed to have come of age. God was slowly banished as a superstitious holdover from the Dark Ages. "Enlightened" people had sufficient understanding of the natural world through reason and science. There was no need for spiritual reality, for gods, angels, or demons. Yet one significant problem remained. If God did not exist, how could one account for the existence of the physical universe? Every worldview, to be comprehensive, must have a creation story.

Darwin and the Rise of Naturalism

Charles Darwin, a famous British botanist, answered this question in 1859. In his classic, *The Origin of Species*, he presented a theory of ultimate origins that excluded a creator God. According to Darwin, living organisms were formed by accident and then evolved into the various creatures that exist today through an unguided process of mutation, "selection," and time. Darwin's origins theory gained acceptance in academic circles throughout Europe and America and continues to be taught in schools worldwide today.

Darwin, according to world-renowned British scientist Richard Dawkins, "made it possible to be an intellectually fulfilled atheist."[1] In other words, Darwin's theory removed the need for belief in even the modest creator-god of deism. As a consequence of Darwin's theory, a new worldview shift was afoot. Deism was replaced by naturalism, which today has become the dominant worldview in the industrial West and in academic and urban centers worldwide. Naturalism (sometimes referred to as secularism, materialism, or scientism) rests on the belief that the universe is composed of one substance and one substance only—physical matter. A spiritual or supernatural realm is either nonexistent or unknowable. The physical universe is a "closed system." Every effect must have a natural cause. Indeed, everything can—and must—be explained through the impersonal workings, chance combinations, and interactions of matter.

In the late nineteenth and twentieth centuries, naturalism spread like wildfire throughout Europe, America, and around the world. It swept through universities and seminaries and came to dominate the natural sciences, law, business, and economics. As we shall see, it also had a profound and disastrous impact on the church.

Naturalism posits a strict division between facts and values. Facts are objective and publicly verifiable. Values, on the other hand, are subjective, personally constructed meanings. Science exists in the realm of fact, in the real world of the five senses—sight, sound, touch, taste, and smell. It is the world where men and women live, breathe, and exist. Religion, spiritual belief, and faith exist in the realm of the personal, subjective, and emotional. Humans learn what is true through human reason and scientific inquiry. The spiritual world is unreal or unknowable; it is the realm of subjective belief and religion; it is the realm of fantasy and make-believe. "At best," explains one observer, "religion paints a coat of 'value' over the otherwise valueless 'facts' disclosed by science."[2] Because naturalism is the dominant worldview of the modern West, this mindset permeates nearly every area of modern life and thought.

Facts
Objective, public reality
Science and reason

Values
Subjective, personal belief
Religion and faith

Naturalism Impacts the Church

As deism, Darwinism, and eventually naturalism gained cultural supremacy, the church in the West was slowly pushed toward the margins of society. To retain a degree of social and cultural influence, many mainline Christian denominations attempted to accommodate these new belief systems, with disastrous consequences. They suppressed the distinctively supernatural, spiritual elements of the biblical worldview. New schools of theology were created to modernize Christian belief so the church could keep pace with changing times. One observer notes, "Contemporary theologians . . . [were] subject to the temptation to understand the Christian faith in light of the dogmas of the Enlightenment, rather than the Enlightenment in the light of the . . . Christian faith."[3]

One modernizing theologian was Friedrich Schleiermacher (1768–1834). Influenced by naturalism's belief that God is either unknowable or unreal, Schleiermacher did not base Christian faith on historically verifiable realities such as the life, death, and resurrection of Jesus. Instead, he rooted Christian faith in subjective human belief. Faith in Christ became a matter of personal experience, rooted in emotional need. It was not a response to an objectively real God who exists and has communicated to mankind reliably through the Bible.[4] Schleiermacher's "Christianity" was little more than a spiritualized version of naturalism, in which science claims the sole authority to describe reality. In this worldview, spiritual belief is considered subjective and is "real" only if an individual believes it to be. Schleiermacher and his fellow theologians formed the beginning of a movement that drastically impacted seminaries and theological schools throughout the West. In time, as students graduated from these schools, they carried these new theological assumptions into church pulpits throughout Europe and America.

The Social Gospel

With God safely locked away in the realm of subjective belief, modern man became a master of his own destiny. For Christians, this meant that God's kingdom could now be realized here on earth through human efforts and knowledge alone. New theologies rejected the biblical doctrine of the Fall and human sinfulness and depravity. Consequently, they downplayed the need for evangelism, repentance, and salvation.

One well-known nineteenth-century American newspaperman, Horace Greeley, spoke for many when he wrote, "The heart of man is not depraved . . . his passions do not prompt to wrong doing, and do not therefore by their actions, produce evil." According to Greeley, "Evil flows only from social repression or subversion. Give [people] full scope, free play, a perfect and complete development, and universal happiness must be the result. . . . Create a new form of Society in which this shall be possible . . . then you will have the perfect Society; then you will have 'the Kingdom of Heaven.'"[5]

The movement that was given birth from these beliefs came to be known as the "social gospel." As Greeley indicated, a core tenant of the movement was the belief that evil was created by the way a society was organized, not by anything innately evil within man.

The Reaction of the Fundamentalists

Such beliefs amounted to heresy in the minds of more orthodox believers, who saw such theological liberalism as directly opposed to the Bible. A countermovement known as fundamentalism was birthed. It sought to rescue the church by emphasizing the spiritual fundamentals of Scripture. It upheld the authority of the Bible as God's supernatural revelation, the incarnation of God in Jesus, and Jesus' atoning death on the cross for human sin.

Naturalism, the enemy of fundamentalism, divided reality into two categories—facts and values—with science and reason claiming the sole capacity to determine truth. Reacting against this, fundamentalists unintentionally borrowed from the ancient Gnostic heresy. Science and reason were looked upon as worldly and secular—things that Christians should avoid. Faith was pitted against reason, the spiritual against the secular. The spiritual realm—the realm of God, the Bible, evangelism, church attendance, "full-time Christian service," and prayer—was seen as good. The physical or material realm was seen as lower and "worldly." Science, human reason, politics, economics, and social action, all dominated by naturalism, were branded as secular—things to be avoided.

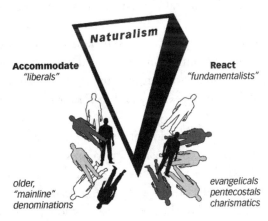

Impact on the World Missions Movement

The fundamentalist movement had a striking impact on global missions. At the time of the fundamentalist reaction to naturalism, hundreds of thousands of Christian missionaries were deployed from Europe and America to the farthest corners of the globe. These missionaries went with great zeal and made incredible sacrifices for the cause of Christ. Yet many were infected with a Gnostic mindset, which they passed on to indigenous believers through the churches they planted. The missionaries associated any missionary activity outside of evangelism and church planting with the Social Gospel movement. Liberal theologians taught that the kingdom of God could be achieved here and now through social action and enlightened government programs. In reaction, fundamentalist and evangelical missionaries taught that the kingdom of God was a strictly spiritual reality, important only in the afterlife.

Separating Social Action from Gospel Proclamation

To the liberal church, humans were masters of their destiny. Human wisdom, expressed through modern science, technology, and enlightened government policy, was sufficient to solve the social, political, and economic problems facing the world. God's role in human affairs was peripheral, limited, and largely irrelevant. Mankind was given responsibility by God to impact society and to conform the social order to the teachings of Christ.

The combination of theological liberalism and social universalism in the United States gave rise to massive government programs after World War II. These programs set out to eliminate poverty at home and abroad. New social policies and large government bureaucracies were created to dispense aid to the poor. It was not long, however, before it became evident that the programs were not succeeding.

The tiny island nation of Haiti provides a sobering case study. Since 1970 thousands of international governmental and nongovernmental aid programs and billions of U.S. dollars have been directed toward healing the economic, social, and spiritual wounds of Haiti's nearly ten million inhabitants. Yet, despite this massive and sustained effort, Haiti remains the most impoverished and broken nation in the Western Hemisphere.

The domestic "war on poverty" in the United States failed just as miserably. Between 1960 and 1990 billions of U.S. dollars were dispensed through welfare programs to people living in poverty. The number of people who lived below the government-established poverty line actually increased during this time period. Because of this, the American welfare system was completely overhauled in the 1990s.

Why did these well-intentioned efforts failed so miserably? Because they ignored the clear biblical teaching that we are a broken people and race. Our best knowledge, resources, and technology will not heal our brokenness. We will remain broken if our efforts do not comply with God's revelation of how we should live—in all areas of life. While the Bible affirms that human reason and the development of resources have a role in our healing, they must be combined with the understanding that humans are sinful and that complete, supernatural healing is available only through the cross of Jesus. Without that understanding, the best intentioned efforts are destined to fail.

Separating Gospel Proclamation from Social Action

While the liberal church was busily working to usher in the kingdom of God through social programs based on human wisdom, the evangelicals were busily ignoring or downplaying the physical needs of the poor and focusing almost exclusively on evangelism and church planting.

For many, "loving God" was viewed as spiritual work and "loving your neighbor" was something that happened in the secular, material world. Over the course of time, this unbiblical dichotomy led many to believe that "God's redemptive work takes place only in the spiritual realm, while the rest of the physical world is seemingly left to the Devil."[6] If evangelicals did minister to physical needs, it was often as "bait," a means to the greater goal of evangelism.

Fundamentalists were using the "lifeboat" metaphor long before it was adopted by the recent secularist lifeboaters. In *Modern Revivalism: From Charles Grandison Finney to Billy Graham*, William McLoughlin reports this quote by Dwight L. Moody: "I look upon this world as a wrecked vessel. God has given me a lifeboat and said to me, 'Moody, save all you can.'"[7] Moody, a devout Christian, was used by God to accomplish great things. Yet such statements reflect an unbiblical dichotomy that places God's interest in saving human souls ahead of his interest in redeeming the rest of creation. Evangelism is central to biblical ministry, but it is only the starting point of the process. The end goal is making disciples of all nations.

This narrow, spiritual-only mindset led to a proliferation of churches around the world today that are characterized by superficiality. Many of these churches are numerically strong but culturally impotent and marginalized, making little or no impact on their surrounding society.

Consequences for Churches Today

Many contemporary Christians, because of this divided mindset, live compartmentalized lifestyles. They live in a "spiritual world" when they are involved with the church, in Bible study or prayer. The rest of the time, particularly in their vocational lives, they live in the "secular world."

This compartmentalization riddles our conversations. For example, it is not uncommon to hear Christians speak about leaving their secular jobs and entering "full-time Christian service," presumably in a church, Christian organization, or the mission field. From this perspective, Christians who are not in full-time Christian service and are working in the secular world are second-class citizens. Believing this, they operate according to the value system of secular culture.[8] The sad result is that God is no longer honored as Lord of all, and the influence of Christians with a biblical worldview is removed from the marketplace.

When Christians adopt the divided mindset instead of the worldview of the Bible, they lose their desire to engage the culture and therefore do not obey Christ's command to "make disciples of all nations." Filling the earth with the knowledge of the Lord (Isa. 11:9) is reduced to filling my heart with the knowledge of the Lord. When the church has this divided mindset, Christians no longer shape media, education, politics, or art. They no longer disciple the nations; rather, they are discipled by the nations. They allow the prevailing trends, beliefs, and practices of the secular world to set the agenda.

We see evidence of this in churches around the world that reflect the priorities and values of the surrounding culture. In America, for example, psychology has replaced theology as the defining language in many evangelical churches, and worship is designed to help church attendees feel good about themselves rather than to magnify the character and works of God. The churches are often measured by the size of their buildings or the number of attendees rather than by how well they manifest the nature and character of God in a broken world or by their impact on society.

With a divided mindset, much of the church today has a muddled understanding of its mission in the world. The comprehensive nature of God's "big agenda"—the redemption of all things that were broken at the Fall—has been lost. Never has there been a time in history when there have been more churches and more professing Christians who are making less of an impact on their surrounding cultures.

Change Is in the Air!

Yet by God's grace this is changing. New ways of thinking are emerging to replace the weak, Gnostic theology of the preceding generation. We find evidence of this through the influential teaching of John Stott and the Lausanne Movement, which has labored mightily to show that there can be no real dichotomy between faith and good works.

Further evidence is seen through the rise of Christian relief and development. Prior to the 1950s there were virtually no evangelical relief and development organizations. Today World Vision, World Relief, World Concern, Food for the Hungry, and other similar groups provide compassionate aid to millions of people in some of the poorest nations on earth. Many churches also are rethinking their mission to the world and, in the process, rediscovering Christ's teachings on the kingdom of God as a vision for comprehensive transformation.

We are living at a *kairos* moment in church history—a pivotal time where old paradigms are giving way and new ones are emerging. God is the Lord of history. He is actively at work in each generation and in every nation to accomplish his grand purpose of advancing his rule and reign on earth—His promise of extending the blessing of Abraham to every tribe, tongue, people, and nation (Gen. 12:3). This purpose won't be fully realized on this side of Christ's return, yet it nevertheless provides present hope for substantial healing in all areas through the finished work of Christ.

⌇ Endnotes

Introduction

1. David Hall, "Life of the Party," *Tabletalk*, October 2002, p. 55.

Session 1

1. Patrick Glynn, "Beyond the Death of God," *National Review*, May 6, 1996, p. 28.
2. Michael J. Behe, *Darwin's Black Box* (New York: Free Press, 1996), pp. 4–5.
3. Ibid., pp. 39, 42.
4. *Holism* is the standard spelling of the word of which *wholism* is a variant spelling. While both words share the same meanings, *holism* has been adopted by, among others, advocates and practitioners of New Age ideas and philosophies. We have adopted the variant spelling to distinguish the biblical concept of wholism from these views and to more clearly show the root word *whole*.
5. J. I. Packer, *Concise Theology: A Guide to Historic Christian Beliefs* (Wheaton, Ill.: Tyndale, 1993), p. 42.
6. Nancy R. Pearcey, *Total Truth: Liberating Christianity from Its Cultural Captivity* (Wheaton, Ill.: Crossway Books, 2004), p. 132.

Session 2

1. Erwin W. Lutzer, *Hitler's Cross* (Chicago: Moody Press, 1995), pp. 11–12.
2. Ibid., p. 104.
3. Ibid., p. 23.
4. Ibid., pp. 110–111.
5. Ibid., p. 111.
6. Ibid.
7. Ibid., p. 132.
8. Ibid, p. 130.
9. Ibid.
10. Ibid, pp. 134–135
11. Ibid, p. 134.
12. Nancy R. Pearcey, *Total Truth: Liberating Christianity from Its Cultural Captivity* (Wheaton, Ill.: Crossway Books, 2004), p. 33.
13. John D. Beckett, *Loving Monday: Succeeding in Business Without Selling Your Soul* (Downers Grove, Ill.: InterVarsity Press, 2001), p. 52.
14. Ibid., pp. 53, 58, 68–69.
15. It should be noted that "religion" is at the root of all public life. Religion can

be understood as a set of presuppositions held by faith. In the West, secularism (or naturalism) forms the "religion" at the root of society. Secularism provided the religious basis for both Nazism in Germany prior to World War II and Communism in the former Soviet Union.

16. Beckett, *Loving Monday*, p. 72.

Session 3

1. Joel Beeke, "Taking Every Thought Captive," *Tabletalk*, October 2002, p. 9.
2. Quoted in John Hendrik DeVries, biographical notes to Abraham Kuyper, *Lectures on Calvinism* (1931; reprint, Grand Rapids: Eerdmans, 1994), p. iii.
3. Chris Strevel, "Not One Square Inch . . . ," *Tabletalk*, October 2002, p. 52.
4. David Hall, "Life of the Party," *Tabletalk*, October 2002, p. 55.
5. Ibid., p. 54.
6. Quoted in Os Guinness, *The Call: Finding and Fulfilling the Central Purpose of Your Life* (Nashville: Word, 1998), p. 34.
7. Grover Gunn, "Making Waves," *Tabletalk*, January 2001, p. 57.
8. Ibid., p. 12.
9. Guinness, *The Call*, pp. 34–35.
10. E. Stanley Jones, *The Unshakable Kingdom and the Unchanging Person* (Nashville: Abingdon, 1972), p. 159.
11. Dallas Willard, *The Divine Conspiracy: Rediscovering Our Hidden Life in God* (San Francisco: HarperSanFrancisco, 1998), p. 27.

Session 4

1. Ruth and Vishal Mangalwadi, *The Legacy of William Carey: A Model for the Transformation of a Culture* (Wheaton, Ill.: Crossway Books, 1999), p. vx.
2. Quoted in ibid., p. 10.
3. Ibid., p. 13.
4. Ibid., p. 24.
5. Ibid., pp. 17–25.
6. Francis A. Schaeffer, *Pollution and the Death of Man: The Christian View of Ecology* (Wheaton, Ill.: Tyndale House, 1970), p. 68.
7. Tetsunao Yamamori, *God's New Envoys: A Bold Strategy for Penetrating "Closed Countries"* (Portland, Ore.: Multnomah, 1987), p. 135.
8. David F. Wells, *No Place for Truth, or, Whatever Happened to Evangelical Theology?* (Grand Rapids: W. B. Eerdmans, 1993), p. 103.

Session 5

1. George Grant, *The Micah Mandate: Balancing the Christian Life* (Nashville: Cumberland House, 1999), p. 241.

2. H. Greeley and H. J. Raymond, *Association Discussed: or, The Socialism of the Tribune Examined* (New York: Harper & Brothers, 1847), p. 66.

3. John Stott, quoted in Rhonda Oosterhoff, "Discipleship Conference Addresses 'Superficiality' in Worldwide Church," *World Pulse*, November 5, 1999, p. 1.

Session 6

1. John Fuellenbach, *The Kingdom of God: The Message of Jesus Today* (New York: Orbis Books, 1995), p. 15.

2. E. Stanley Jones, *The Unshakable Kingdom and the Unchanging Person* (Nashville: Abingdon Press, 1972), p. 19.

3. John Stott, *New Issues Facing Christians Today* (London: Marshall Pickering, 1999), p. 36.

4. Douglas Layton, *Our Father's Kingdom: The Church and the Nations* (Nashville: World Impact, 2000), p. 20.

5. Quoted in Greg Bailey, "Love Fulfills the Law," *Tabletalk*, November 2002, p. 26.

6. Dallas Willard, *The Divine Conspiracy: Rediscovering Our Hidden Life in God* (San Francisco: HarperSanFrancisco, 1998), pp. 22–23.

7. John Piper, *Brothers, We Are Not Professionals: A Plea to Pastors for Radical Ministry* (Nashville: Broadman & Holman, 2002), p. 11.

8. Ibid.

Appendix

1. Richard Dawkins, *The Blind Watchmaker* (New York: Norton, 1986), p. 6.

2. John F. Haught, "The Darwinian Struggle: Catholics, Pay Attention," *Commonwealth*, September 24, 1999, pp. 14–16.

3. John H. Leith, *Crisis in the Church: The Plight of Theological Education* (Louisville, Ky.: Westminster John Knox, 1997), p. 36.

4. Iain H. Murray, *Evangelicalism Divided: A Record of Crucial Change in the Years 1950 to 2000* (Carlisle, Pa.: Banner of Truth Trust, 2000), p. 7.

5. *New York Courier and Enquirer*, April 16, 1847, and March 5, 1847, quoted in Marvin Olasky, *The Tragedy of American Compassion* (Wheaton, Ill.: Crossway Books, 1992), p. 54.

6. Bryant L. Myers, *Walking with the Poor* (Maryknoll, N.Y.: Orbis Books, 1999), p. 6.

7. William McLoughlin, *Modern Revivalism: From Charles Grandison Finney to Billy Graham* (New York: Ronald Press, 1959), p. 257.

8. For a more detailed treatment of this subject, see Darrow L. Miller, *LifeWork: A Biblical Theology for What You Do Every Day* (Seattle: YWAM Publishing, 2009).

⌒ Leader's Guide

We suggest the following guidelines for people leading study groups through this Bible study. Of course you will need to adapt the studies and our suggestions to your particular group and culture.

Preparing for and Facilitating a Group

- We suggest meeting for one hour per session. This will allow:
  - ❖ 20 minutes to review the Key Verses and Biblical Insights sections.
  - ❖ 20 minutes to discuss the Discovery Questions and Personal Application sections.
  - ❖ 10 minutes to pray for one another.
  - ❖ 10 minutes for general prayer and worship.
- To ensure that everyone contributes to the conversation, it's best to keep the group at six to eight participants (no more than twelve). If the membership increases, consider splitting into smaller groups during the discussion times and coming back together for concluding prayer.
- If group members have their own books, ask them to complete the session individually before they attend the meeting.
- To guide the group effectively, complete each session yourself before you meet together. Make sure you understand the main points of each session. Think about how they apply to your own life. Then, as you lead the group, you can better facilitate the discussion by clarifying the questions when needed and offering suggestions if the conversation lags.
- For each meeting, arrive ahead of time to prepare the location (chairs, refreshments, teaching aids, etc.) and to greet group members as they arrive.
- For your first meeting, be sure to take time to introduce each group member. You may wish to do an activity that will help group members get to know each other. Introduce the study by presenting key ideas from the Introduction and reading the overall objectives for the sessions (listed in the Study Notes following this Leader's Guide).

◆ Be a *facilitator*, not a teacher. Here are some suggestions:

  ❖ Encourage group participation. Sitting in a circle (rather than rows) can help.

  ❖ Use group members' names.

  ❖ Ask different people to pray and read.

  ❖ Ask questions and wait for answers. Don't immediately give your own answer.

  ❖ Thank group members for their ideas, and ask others what they think.

  ❖ Draw out members who need encouragement to speak up.

  ❖ Tactfully redirect the focus from participants who tend to dominate the discussion.

  ❖ Ask participants for explanation when they give simple "yes" or "no" answers.

  ❖ Pace your study at a rate that allows for group members' maximum understanding. Review as often as necessary.

  ❖ Keep the session objective in mind as you work through the session. These objectives, as well as possible responses for questions, are listed in the Study Notes.

Suggestions for Leading Each Session

◆ Have a group member open and close each meeting time with prayer.

◆ Begin the meeting by reviewing the Key Points to Remember from the previous session. Take time to discuss how group members may have applied the teaching from the previous session since the last meeting.

◆ You may wish to assign the Key Verses to Read as a memorization exercise. If so, take time at the beginning of the session to allow group members to recite the verses corresponding to the session. This can easily be done in pairs to save time.

◆ Refer back to the Key Words to Know section as necessary during discussion.

◆ Read the Key Verses to Read and answer the questions provided as a group. (See possible responses to these questions in the Study Notes.)

◆ If each group member has a book, take turns reading the Biblical

Insights section together. If you're the only one with a book, share the main points or read this section to the group. The Key Points to Remember section will help present the main ideas.

♦ Answer and discuss the Discovery Questions together as a group. (See possible responses to these questions in the Study Notes.)

♦ Answer and discuss the Personal Application questions together as a group. If group members have their own books, you may wish to break up into smaller groups (two to three people) and have each subgroup read and answer the Personal Application questions.

♦ You will find the session Objectives, Possible Responses to Questions for Key Verses to Read, and Possible Responses to Discovery Questions for each session in the Study Notes that follow this Leader's Guide.

Study Notes

Whether you lead or participate in a small group or study alone, you may find it helpful to consult the session objectives and suggested responses for each session's Key Verses to Read and Discovery questions. Not all questions have a "right" or "wrong" answer, but these suggestions will help stimulate your thinking.

Session One: Understanding Wholism

Objective: To define the biblical concept of wholism and explain how it relates to God, the church, and the Bible.

Possible Responses to Questions for Key Verses to Read

1. The church
2. Apostles, prophets, teachers, miracle workers, those with gifts of healing, those with gifts of helping others, those with gifts of administration, and those able to speak in different tongues
3. With no division, every part having equal concern for the other

Possible Responses to Discovery Questions

1. Truth and love
2. If we lose truth, our witness becomes empty and powerless. If we lose love, our witness becomes heartless crusading.
3. Preaching, teaching, and healing
4. Our ministry loses its effectiveness in advancing the kingdom of God and fails to measure up to Christ's example.
5. Compassionate, gracious, slow to anger, loving, faithful, forgiving, just
6. We fail to have a complete or accurate view of God.
7. Faith in God and doing good works/deeds
8. Our faith becomes empty and meaningless.

Session Two: The Divided Mind and Life

Objective: To reveal the unbiblical separation in everyday life and culture between the spiritual and secular realms, and to define the biblical, comprehensive view of discipleship.

Possible Responses to Questions for Key Verses to Read

1. The imagery of warfare. This imagery conveys a sense of life-and-death seriousness. Illusions to warfare are appropriate because our lives are caught up in a very real cosmic battle between God and Satan.
2. We are to take captive "every thought" to make them "obedient" to, or in line with, the teachings of Christ.
3. No. Jesus is both Creator and Lord of all. Therefore, we need to think about all aspects of life from the vantage point of scriptural truth.
4. We can become disciplined students of the Bible, God's Word, and work to apply its truth.

Possible Responses to Discovery Questions

1. Leaving our former way of life and following Jesus wherever he leads.
2. Leaving everything behind for the sake of Christ.
3. Because he is the Supreme Authority in the universe.
4. He gave up his status as a respected religious leader in the Jewish community. Compared to gaining Christ, he describes what he gave up as "rubbish" (worthless).
5. It involves denying yourself, your self-will, your dreams and plans for the future, and your prerogatives and giving yourself, your life, and your future wholly over to Christ's purposes.
6. By giving our lives wholly over to Christ to use for his purposes.
7. He desired to "inherit eternal life." Jesus told him to "sell everything you have and give it to the poor." The young man was not willing to pay that price.
8. Because riches function as an idol or false God in their lives. The rich are often unwilling to give up their riches for the sake of Christ.

Session Three: Living with Wholism in Mind

Objective: To show how, in the lives of Jesus' followers, faith can and should be integrated into every area of life.

Possible Responses to Questions for Key Verses to Read

1. They both contain the phrases "whatever you do" and "do it all." In 1 Corinthians 10:31, the example is "eating and drinking." In Colossians 3:17, the focus is on whatever you do in "word or deed." Likewise, in 1 Corinthians 10:31, we are to "do it all" for the glory of God. In Colossians 3:17 we are to "do it all" in the name of the Lord Jesus, giving thanks to God.
2. Everything we do—every word we speak, every deed we do—even eating and drinking.
3. Because they are simple, everyday, "unspiritual" tasks. They set a high bar. If "eating and drinking" are not excluded from tasks done for God's glory, than nothing else is.
4. It shows us that everything in creation was made by God and nothing is outside his control or care. So all of our actions in creation should be to the glory of God.

Possible Responses to Discovery Questions

1. He is the "owner" of the earth and everything in it.
2. Isaiah saw the Lord seated on a throne, high and exalted. The vision reveals that God is perfectly holy and that the whole earth is full of his glory.
3. God's dominion is eternal and his kingdom endures from generation to generation. He does as he pleases with the powers of heaven and the peoples of the earth. No one can hold back his hand.
4. Jesus exercises authority over everything and everyone. His authority is exercised presently as well as eternally.
5. This parable teaches that there is an enemy who is sowing evil. God allows this evil to exist side by side with the good for the present, but in the future the evil will be destroyed.
6. God purchased us.
7. For God, the price was the life of his "only begotten Son." For Jesus, the price was his own life—his blood shed on the cross.
8. We owe him our bodies—our entire lives—as living sacrifices.
9. Jesus' relationship to his Father was one of love and complete obedience.

Session Four: Wholistic Ministry

Objective: To show how ministry as God intended it advances God's kingdom and addresses every relationship broken through the Fall.

Possible Responses to Questions for Key Verses to Read

1. Preaching, teaching, and healing
2. The advancement of God's kingdom—God's will being done "on earth as it is in heaven"
3. No; all parts are necessary. If any part were removed, the accomplishment of the overall goal would be compromised.

Possible Responses to Discovery Questions

1. The primary relationship is the relationship between God and mankind. It is primary because of the special, unique relationship between God and man. In all creation, only man (men and women) is made in the image and likeness of God.
2. Humans are image-bearers of God, created by God to exercise dominion and stewardship over creation.
3. Man with his fellow man (human-to-human relationships).
4. Man with creation/the physical environment
5. The primary relationship was broken. Adam and Eve "hid" from God and were "afraid" of him.
6. Conflict entered into the secondary relationship between Adam and Eve. Adam blamed Eve for his sin. Likewise, the ground was cursed. From this time forward, Adam would have to work hard for the earth to produce. "Through painful toil you will eat of it."
7. God's response is to redeem all things, including all of these broken relationships. Christ died on the cross to redeem "all things."
8. We have been given the ministry of reconciliation. We are to be God's "ambassadors," calling on the world to be reconciled to God through Christ.
9. We can "preach" or speak the truth revealed in Scripture about God, sin, and redemption. We can also love others with the love of Christ. We can share what we have with those in need and be concerned for the comprehensive welfare of others.

10. God's redemptive plan will be accomplished at the end of the age when God creates "a new heaven and a new earth." There will be no more alienation between God and man. "The dwelling of God will be with men, and he will live with them. They will be his people, and God himself will be with them and be their God." There will be no more hunger, sorrow, or pain.

Session Five: Obstacles to Wholistic Ministry

Objective: To describe dualistic and materialistic views in the church that oppose or hinder biblical, wholistic ministry.

Possible Responses to Questions for Key Verses to Read

1. Preaching the Word (correcting, rebuking, and encouraging) and loving with actions
2. He warned against loving with word only, without actions.
3. If we neglect the Word, we lose God's truth needed for salvation and fullness of life. Yet if we only speak God's words and don't demonstrate the truth with our lives and actions, it may be empty and meaningless to those who hear, particularly those with profound physical needs.

Possible Responses to Discovery Questions

1. (1) Do not conform to the patterns of this world; (2) be transformed by the renewing of your mind; (3) then you will understand God's will for your life.
2. A caterpillar is transformed into a butterfly. To be transformed means to be completely changed at every level and in every way.
3. My mind must be transformed.
4. "Hold to" (believe and live out) the teachings of Jesus.
5. IF you hold to my teachings, THEN you will know the truth and the truth will set you free.
6. To practice wholistic ministry, we must understand the truth about God, human nature, creation, the fall, and redemption. We must understand the "big picture" of God's entire revelation in Scripture. We can only understand these things if we are devoted students of God's Word and if we hold to the teachings of Jesus.

7. Yes.
8. We must confess our sin to God. He is "faithful and just and will forgive us our sins and purify us from all unrighteousness."

Session Six: Wholistic Ministry Essentials

Objective: To define key aspects of wholistic ministry, which seeks to glorify God and advance his kingdom.

Possible Responses to Questions for Key Verses to Read

1. In wisdom, in stature, in favor with God, and in favor with man
2. We grow in wisdom as we gain knowledge and understanding of God's Word and live it out in our lives. We grow in stature (physically) through proper nutrition and exercise. We grow in favor with God as we trust in Jesus as our Savior and Lord and live as his disciples. We grow in favor with man as we obey the biblical commands to love and serve others as we love ourselves and have lives characterized by humility, integrity, and joy.
3. It is significant because it shows us that all four areas are equally critical for development. I must be concerned about all four areas for my own growth and development as well as for the growth and development of others.
4. It was a process.

Possible Responses to Discovery Questions

1. Jesus was sent "to preach the good news of the kingdom of God." This tells us that the kingdom of God was Christ's main message and was deeply on his heart.
2. He came to his final hour to bring glory to God. This was his ultimate purpose: to glorify the name of God. This ought to be our ultimate purpose as well.
3. Harmony will exist throughout creation. The earth will be full of the knowledge of the Lord. There will be no more sorrow, hunger, or death.
4. When we care for broken, hurting people, we show care and love for God.

5. Defending the cause of the weak and fatherless. Maintaining the rights of the poor and oppressed. Rescuing the weak and needy from the wicked. Working against injustice and setting the oppressed free. Sharing food with the hungry and providing the poor with shelter. Clothing the naked and looking after orphans and widows.

6. People need God's Word (the truth) and Jesus. We need both physical and spiritual food because we are a seamless combination of body and soul. We will go "hungry" if one or the other is neglected—literally or spiritually.

7. We are to carry out ministry in total dependence on God and his strength and power. We are "cursed" if we trust in men or in our own strength.

8. The ultimate purpose of our ministry is to glorify God. We do that when we serve "with the strength God provides."

≈ About the Author

Scott D. Allen is president of Disciple Nations Alliance support office in Phoenix, Arizona. After receiving his bachelor's degree in history from Willamette University in Salem, Oregon, in 1988, Scott joined Food for the Hungry International, where he served until 2007. Along with Darrow Miller and Bob Moffitt, Scott helped launch the Disciple Nations Alliance. He has authored and coauthored a number of books, including *The Forest in the Seed: A Biblical Perspective on Resources and Development* and *Against All Hope: Hope for Africa*. Scott lives with his wife, Kim, and their five children in Phoenix, Arizona.

Other **KINGDOM LIFESTYLE** Bible Studies

Revolutionizing Lives and Renewing Minds!

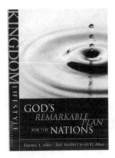

God's Remarkable Plan for the Nations
by Scott D. Allen, Darrow L. Miller, and Bob Moffitt

God's redemptive plan is the central theme of the entire Bible, from Genesis to Revelation. While this plan begins with individuals, it's more comprehensive—more wonderful—than this. God's redemptive interest extends to the healing and transformation of entire nations and cultures, undercutting injustice, poverty, and corruption and encompassing every sphere of society, from commerce to the arts to government. Will the church in our generation be faithful to Jesus' command to make disciples of all nations according to the fullness of what he intended? For this to occur, we must regain a comprehensive understanding of God's remarkable plan for the nations—a plan that touches our lives profoundly. ISBN 978-1-57658-352-4

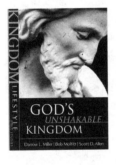

God's Unshakable Kingdom
by Scott D. Allen, Darrow L. Miller, and Bob Moffitt

The concept of the kingdom of God is one of the most confusing and misunderstood ideas in the Bible. Yet it's indisputable that the kingdom of God was central to Jesus' teachings. As he ministered, Jesus talked passionately about the kingdom. The phrase "kingdom of God" or "kingdom of heaven" appears ninety-eight times in the New Testament and is used more than sixty times by Jesus. This profound study explores the kingdom of God, helping believers build a biblical understanding of the vision for which Jesus lived and died—a vision that transforms individuals, families, churches, and whole nations. ISBN 978-1-57658-346-3

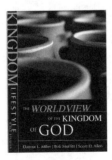

The Worldview of the Kingdom of God
by Scott D. Allen, Darrow L. Miller, and Bob Moffitt

Today, there are more churches and more Christians in the world than at any time in history. But to what end? Poverty and corruption thrive in developing countries that have been evangelized. Moral and spiritual poverty reign in the "Christian" West. Why? Because believers don't have the "mind of Christ." All of us have a worldview, or a mental model of the world. This set of ideas and assumptions ultimately determines the choices we make and the kind of lives we lead. The Worldview of the Kingdom of God explores the biblical worldview and why understanding it and living it out are essential to leading a fruitful, abundant life. ISBN 978-1-57658-351-7

Disciple Nations Alliance

Founded by:
Harvest and Food for
the Hungry International

Equipping the Church to Transform the World

The Disciple Nations Alliance is a movement of individuals, churches, and organizations with a common vision: to see the global church rise to her full potential as God's instrument for the healing, blessing, and transformation of the nations.

The Disciple Nations Alliance was founded in 1997 through a partnership between Food for the Hungry (www.fh.org) and Harvest (www.harvestfoundation. org). Its mission is to influence the paradigm and practice of local churches around the world, helping them to recognize and replace false beliefs with a robust biblical worldview—bringing truth, justice, and beauty into every sphere of society—and to demonstrate Christ's love in practical ways, addressing the brokenness in their communities and nations beginning with their own resources.

For more information about the Disciple Nations Alliance as well as access to a host of resources, curricula, books, study materials, and application tools, please visit our website: www.disciplenations.org.

Disciple Nations Alliance

1110 E Missouri Ave, Ste. 393, Phoenix, Arizona 85014
www.disciplenations.org
E-mail: info@disciplenations.org

Samaritan Strategy Africa

The messages and teaching contained in the Kingdom Lifestyle Bible Studies are being championed throughout the continent of Africa through the efforts of Samaritan Strategy Africa, a collaborative network of African churches and Christian organizations that have banded together to accomplish the urgent goal of awakening, equipping, and mobilizing the African church to rise up and transform society. Through training, mentoring, conferences, and publications, Samaritan Strategy Africa aims to help churches

- discover God's vision of comprehensive healing and transformation of the nations;
- adopt a biblical worldview and then live it out by taking truth, goodness, and beauty into every sphere of society; and
- practice a ministry of outreach within the community, demonstrating Christ's love to needy and broken people through works of service.

If you would like more information about Samaritan Strategy Africa, including upcoming training events and how you, your church, or your organization can be involved, we invite you to visit our website or contact us.

Samaritan Strategy Africa

Dennis Tongoi, Team Leader
PO Box 40360-00100
Nairobi, Kenya
Phone: 254-20-2720037/56
E-mail: afg@cms-africa.org
Website: www.samaritan-strategy-africa.org

Samaritan Strategy Africa is affiliated with the Disciple Nations Alliance (DNA), a global movement founded in 1997 through a partnership between Food for the Hungry and Harvest. DNA exists to see engaged, credible, high-impact local churches effecting real transformation in their communities and in sufficient mass to disciple their nations. For more information, visit www.disciplenations.org.